WOMEN AND
PUBLIC POLICIES

WOMEN AND
PUBLIC POLICIES

Joyce Gelb
and
Marian Lief Palley

Princeton University Press
Princeton, New Jersey

Copyright © 1982 by Princeton University Press

Published by Princeton University Press,
41 William Street, Princeton, New Jersey
In the United Kingdom: Princeton University Press,
Guildford, Surrey

All Rights Reserved

Library of Congress Cataloging in Publication Data will be
found on the last printed page of this book

This book has been composed in Linotron Sabon

Clothbound editions of Princeton University Press books
are printed on acid-free paper, and binding materials are
chosen for strength and durability

Printed in the United States of America by Princeton
University Press, Princeton, New Jersey

To Howard and Joe, who have helped to reform today's society, and to Andrew, Elizabeth, Jonathan, and Steve, who we hope will live in a more equitable society.

CONTENTS

List of Tables ix
List of Abbreviations xi
Preface xiii

Chapter 1: Feminism and the American Political System 3

Chapter 2: Feminist Mobilization 14

Chapter 3: The Group Actors: Resources and Strategies 37

Chapter 4: Women and Credit Discrimination 63

Chapter 5: Title IX: The Politics of Sex Discrimination 95

Chapter 6: Women Divided among Themselves: "The Right to Life" versus "Free Choice" 125

Chapter 7: The Pregnancy Disability Act and Coalition Politics 154

Chapter 8: The Feminist Movement: The Past and Likely Future 167

Appendix 1: Interviews 183
Appendix 2: Questionnaire for Groups and Individuals 187

Index 189

LIST OF TABLES

1. Membership of Traditional Women's Groups
   (1980)   27
2. Feminist Groups' Membership and Staff Resources
   (1978)   28
3. Professional Salaries (1979)   41
4. Major Sources of Revenue (1978)   44
5. Ford Foundation Grants (1978)   46
6. Interlocking Directorates among Feminist Groups
   (1978)   62
7. Universities and Colleges Offering Sports
   Programs, by Size and Availability of Football
   (1973-74, 1977-78, 1978-79)   101
8. Athletes, Budgets, and Per Capita Expenditures at
   AIAW and NCAA Colleges (1978)   106
9. Should the Right to Have an Abortion Be Left
   Entirely to the Woman and Her Doctor?   143

LIST OF ABBREVIATIONS

AAUP – American Association of University Professors
AAUW – American Association of University Women
ACE – American Council on Education
ACLU – American Civil Liberties Union
ACLU-RFP – Reproductive Freedom Project
ACLU-WRP – Women's Rights Project
AIAW – Association for Intercollegiate Athletics for Women
BPW – Business and Professional Women
CARASA – Committee for Abortion Rights and Against Sterilization Abuse
CLASP-WRP – Center for Law and Social Policy— Women's Rights Project
CWPS – Center for Women Policy Studies
ECOA – Equal Credit Opportunity Act
EEOC – Equal Employment Opportunities Commission
ERA – Equal Rights Amendment
GFWC – General Federation of Women's Clubs
HEW – Department of Health, Education, and Welfare
IUE – International Union of Electrical, Radio, and Machine Workers
LWV – League of Women Voters
NAACP – National Association for the Advancement of Colored People
NARAL – National Abortion Rights Action League
NCAA – National Collegiate Athletic Association
NCJW – National Council of Jewish Women
NOW – National Organization for Women
NOW-LDEF – Legal Defense and Education Fund

NWPC – National Women's Political Caucus
OCR – Office of Civil Rights, HEW
PAC – Political Action Committee
PEER – Project on Equal Education Rights (of NOW-LDEF)
RCAR – Religious Coalition for Abortion Rights
UAW – United Auto Workers
WEAL – Women's Equity Action League
WEEA – Women's Educational Equity Act
WLDF – Women's Legal Defense Fund

PREFACE

Though the contemporary role of women in American politics
has evolved gradually from the early years of the abolitionist
and suffragist movements to the present era of equal rights
legislation, it is certainly the past twenty years that have seen
the most rapid acceleration in the demands of women's groups
on the political system. In this book we examine four policy
areas—credit, education, abortion, and pregnancy disability—
that have been pursued by the women's movement with well-
developed and articulated political demands. In particular, we
consider why groups are successful or unsuccessful in having
their political demands met, and we try to generalize several
rules for emergent groups to follow from the four case studies.
In addition, we examine the internal workings of the women's
movement so as to gain a better sense of its role in American
politics. Our study focuses on the decade of the 1970s. Thus
the policy and program retrenchments of the Reagan administration are not discussed in this volume.

Many people assisted us during the years we worked on
this book. We presented portions of our research as papers
at several professional meetings, including the American Political Science Association, the Northeast Political Science Association, the Midwest Political Science Association, and the
Western Political Science Association. Often our fellow participants provided us with useful criticisms. In addition, we
published two articles that addressed some of the questions
raised in this volume. One article appeared in the *Journal of
Politics* and the other in the *American Politics Quarterly*.
Reviewers for these two manuscripts provided us with in-
sightful critiques that strengthened this book, too. Gelb presented some of this work to the Columbia University Program
on Sex Roles and Social Change, and Palley introduced some

of this volume's materials to the University of Delaware Women's Studies Colloquium Series.

Several individuals were particularly helpful to us as we wrote the book. We especially want to thank Janet Boles, Irene Diamond, and Michael Hayes, who each critically read the manuscript in its entirety more than once. Leslie Goldstein also reviewed sections of it. The Honorable Ruth Bader Ginsburg provided many useful suggestions.

We received several grants to assist in this project. Gelb received assistance from the National Endowment for the Humanities. She was a recipient of an NEH Category B Fellowship in 1979-80 and a grant from the Project on Non-Profit Organizations, Institute for Social and Policy Studies, Yale University during 1979-80. Portions of the research for Chapters 2 and 3 were supported by the Yale University grant. Palley received funding from the College of Arts and Science of the University of Delaware to assist in the writing and preparation of the manuscript.

The book, in its various drafts, was typed by Jeanne Grill, Gladys Hartman, and Sophia Hoobler. Finally, we would like to thank Sandy Thatcher of Princeton University Press for his continuing encouragement to us as we worked to complete this project.

WOMEN AND
PUBLIC POLICIES

CHAPTER 1

FEMINISM
AND THE AMERICAN
POLITICAL SYSTEM

INTRODUCTION

Students of American politics have long recognized the existence of a "mobilization of bias" that limits access to power
for new "out-groups" on the political scene. According to
E. E. Schattschneider, political systems and subsystems develop a "mobilization of bias," a set of predominant values,
beliefs, rituals, and institutional procedures that operate systematically and consistently to the benefit of certain groups
and at the expense of others. Defenders of the status quo
occupy key positions of power, from which they promote their
vested interests. Schattschneider called attention to the narrow
scope and bias of the American system, stressing the difficulties
present for groups seeking to expand their participation and
increase their impact on policy.[1]

Nonetheless, within the past two decades a plethora of new
groups have appeared to press their demands on the policy-
making process. Among these are groups representing the interests of racial and ethnic minorities, the poor, the aged,
consumers, and environmentalists. In addition, after some fifty
years of dormancy, a feminist movement emerged in the late
1960s and 1970s, and in the brief fifteen years of its existence
this movement, rooted in the middle and upper-middle classes

[1] E. E. Schattschneider, *The Semisovereign People* (New York: Holt, Rinehart
and Winston, 1956), 71, quoted in Peter Bachrach and Morton Baratz, *Power
and Poverty* (New York: Oxford University Press, 1970), 43.

of society, has developed a sophisticated organizational structure and has established itself as a significant presence in national policy making. The evolution of a strong feminist presence in national politics parallels the expansion of interest-group activity in general in Washington. The decade of the 1970s witnessed an increase in the number of organized interests coming to the nation's capital to make demands on the political system. This development seems to have been propelled by an expanding federal role in politics and by an apparent decline in the role of political parties with a concomitant increase in constituency and group influences on members of Congress.

Despite references to *the* feminist movement, it is important to understand at the outset of this analysis that there are numerous components within what is popularly described as the feminist movement, and these multiple groups are referred to as "the movement" merely for the sake of convenience. Feminism is defined here as a movement seeking to operationalize self-determination for women in political, economic, and social roles. In the succeeding chapters the role of women in affecting national public policies during the decade of the 1970s will be considered. Thus the focus of this book is on politics and on the groups active in the political process.

In this study we are concerned more with group leadership behavior than with mass membership behavior. This focus is determined by the predominance of leadership as opposed to mass membership groups in the organized feminist movement. There is, however, broad support for the goals of the feminist movement even though formal membership in most of the primary feminist interest groups is relatively small.

There are four major types of groups that comprise the feminist political community as it is discussed here: mass-based feminist organizations, single-issue groups, specialized litigation and research organizations, and the traditional women's groups such as the League of Women Voters. The group actors will be considered in detail in Chapter 2.

It is our contention that feminists in politics have conformed

4

to both the scope and bias of the system and simultaneously, by virtue of their presence and demands, have expanded the range of decision making to include a broader segment of the populace. Feminists are not inclined to rely on public agitation in order to achieve their goals; rather, they support changes in social policy through conventional lobbying efforts. Feminist groups are represented by "movement" women who share a commitment to changing discriminatory social and economic policies albeit through reformist as opposed to radical techniques. Feminist advocates in Washington are thoroughgoing professionals who maintain a visible presence on a variety of issues. Their reputation for legal and technical expertise coupled with tenacity has gained them access to policy makers at all levels. For example, they are often consulted by federal agencies when regulations are being written, though their clout does not always equal that of their rivals. In contrast, feminists have had an uncertain history in the federal courts, which have pursued ambivalent and often contradictory approaches to issues of sex discrimination. Although some issues raised and advocated by women's groups have prevailed in the courts, the Supreme Court's rejection of the race/sex analogy has meant that feminists have had to develop strategies different from those of civil rights groups that preceded them in several areas under discussion here.

We will demonstrate that feminists can claim primary credit for a series of successes in the adoption and implementation of policies including the Equal Credit Opportunity Act of 1974, the Pregnancy Disability Act of 1978, and Title IX of the Education Amendment of 1972. When they are most successful, feminists participate in broad-based coalitions in which often they play pivotal roles. Increasingly, playing the game of coalition politics, with several coalitions organized around specific issues, has been of major importance to feminists' success.

In addition to the policies analyzed in depth here, feminists have either benefited from or influenced other equal rights legislation related to women. Thus the Equal Pay Act of 1963,

Title VII of the Civil Rights Act of 1964, which makes sex-based discrimination in employment unlawful, Executive Order 11246 (September 1965), amended by Executive Order 11375 of October 1967, prohibiting discrimination in employment under federal contracts, and a prohibition against sex discrimination in mortgage lending in the Fair Housing Act of 1974 all have aided women. In the area of federally funded child care, since President Nixon's veto of the Comprehensive Child Development Act of 1971, which would have brought day care within reach of all families, efforts to gain congressional passage of even a scaled-down measure have been defeated. However, the Tax Reform Act of 1976 does provide a maximum child-care deduction of $400 for one child or $800 for two or more children.

Feminists have also devoted considerable resources and energy to the struggle for the ratification of the Equal Rights Amendment (ERA). The amendment passed Congress easily in 1972, after a fifty-year period of seeking a constitutional amendment to advocate equal rights for women, but has faltered in the state ratification process (after early success in gaining ratification in 35 of the 38 needed states). Nonetheless, feminists did gain a major victory again in Congress when, in 1979, they were able to persuade Congress to extend the deadline for ratification of the ERA for another three years. It does seem unlikely, however, that the amendment will be ratified by the necessary number of states to ensure enactment.

SCOPE OF THE BOOK

The role of women in effecting changes in four separate policy areas—credit, education, pregnancy disability, and free choice regarding abortion—will be considered in this study. Other issues could have been selected, but these four were chosen because they provide a particularly good mix of feminist experiences from an organizational and political perspective.

We will discuss each of the four in separate chapters as they took shape in specific legislation and administrative regulations. Thus the case of credit will be presented within the context of the Equal Credit Opportunity Act of 1974; education will be discussed by focusing on Title IX of the Education Amendments of 1972; pregnancy disability will be highlighted by consideration of the Pregnancy Disability Act of 1978 (Amendments to Title VII of the Civil Rights Act of 1964); and the discussion of free choice regarding abortion will center on the annual Hyde Amendments for the years 1976-1979 (these are amendments to the annual appropriations for the Department of Health, Education, and Welfare and the Department of Labor). Each of the issues selected for study is broadly representative of the policy-making process since each deals with legislative and administrative enactments and their interpretation by regulatory and judicial authorities. From the analysis of specific cases, we will determine which issues and strategies are most likely to produce success for feminists in the political process and will specify the parameters of such success. Before looking at the actual policies, we will examine the major feminist groups that have been especially central to the public policy efforts put forth by women in the past decade.

For each issue discussed, the analysis will include: the underlying problem the issue addresses; the nature of the goal sought; the organizational structure of the feminist movement; efforts at coalition-building both within and outside the feminist movement; the existence of a countermovement to oppose feminist interests; and the interactions of feminist groups within the policy process. We contend that when an issue is perceived as one affecting *role equity* rather than *role change*,[2] success is most likely.

Role equity issues are those policies which extend rights now enjoyed by other groups (men, other minorities) to women and which appear to be relatively delineated or narrow in their implications, permitting policy makers to seek advantage

[2] The terms "role change" and "role equity" were suggested by Maren Lockwood Carden, *Feminism in the Mid-1970's* (New York: Ford Foundation, 1977), 40-43.

with feminist groups and voters with little cost or controversy. In contrast, role change issues appear to produce change in the dependent female role of wife, mother, and homemaker, holding out the potential of greater sexual freedom and independence in a variety of contexts. The latter issues are fraught with greater political pitfalls, including perceived threats to existing values, in turn creating visible and often powerful opposition.

The analysis is based largely on interviews with participants in the policy-making process who have affected the enactment of the laws considered. They include members of Congress and their aides and members of executive agencies and their staffs. In addition, lobbyists and advocates for both the "women's movement" and its opponents, including the anti-abortion "right-to-life" movement, the credit and insurance industry, and the professional athletic community have been interviewed. The interviews were not intended to achieve a quantitative portrait of policy inputs and outputs, but rather to aid in understanding the nature of the policy-making process. (See Appendices 1 and 2 for a sample questionnaire and list of persons interviewed.)

THE THEORETICAL APPROACH

In this study the role of women in politics will be examined from the vantage point of the convergence of contemporary interest-group theory and social-movement theory.[3] It is our belief that emergent groups in American politics such as the feminist movement provide a unique example of both political mobilization and interest-group development. To examine the feminist movement without examining this convergence would be to provide an incomplete analysis of this important group.

Those techniques which appear most effective in achieving even limited change for emergent groups like the feminist

---

[3] This convergence was suggested to the authors in remarks made by Terry Moe at the Annual Meeting of the Western Political Science Association, Denver, Colorado, March 26, 1981.

movement will be analyzed: Does a new group seem to achieve the greatest gains by adhering to traditional tactics, including interest-group lobbying, or is a more radical threat to the "system" more effective in achieving change? Is it reasonable to anticipate fundamental changes in the status quo, or is incremental change the only likely result of reformist political challenge? In addition, we will assess the importance of a mass constituency for groups seeking to effect social change, as well as the constraints placed upon such groups by limited economic resources. The relevance of increased campaign and electoral activity will be considered as well.

Though we suggest a systematic set of rules indicating the kinds of issues, necessary organizational structures and coalition partners, degree of opposition, and techniques likely to produce even marginal political gains for new political groups, it should be emphasized that we are *not* discussing the development of a systematic causal model for either group formation or group behavior. Rather, we will consider those behavioral patterns which, based on the experiences of the contemporary feminist movement, are most likely to facilitate success for emergent groups trying to positively effect changes in the status quo.

More specifically, there are four rules that an emergent group must follow effectively in order to influence public policy:

1. To be effective in American politics, groups must be perceived as legitimate.[4]
2. In order to appear legitimate, groups will find it necessary to focus on incremental issues.[5] In this regard,

---

[4] See David Truman, *The Governmental Process* (New York: Knopf, 1951); Robert Dahl, *A Preface to Democratic Theory* (Chicago: University of Chicago Press, 1956); David J. O'Brien, *Neighborhood Organization and Interest Group Processes* (Princeton: Princeton University Press, 1975).

[5] Charles E. Lindblom, "Still Muddling, Not Yet Through," *Public Administration Review* 39 (Nov./Dec. 1979), 517-26; Theodore Marmor, *The Politics of Medicare* (Chicago: Aldine, 1970), 14-16.

role equity issues are less threatening than role change issues.

3. In order to appear legitimate, groups will stress the provision of information[6] and concentrate on mobilizing their allies. They will seek to avoid confrontation that comes from the use of protest tactics. They will form policy networks, and they will be willing to define success in terms of "increments."

4. Like other conventional interest groups, emergent groups will engage in a struggle over the definition of the situation. This struggle will almost always involve the manipulation of symbols favorable to one's cause. At times, these symbols will be employed to socialize conflict. At other times, symbols will be used to privatize conflict (for example, by defining the issue as one involving just role *equity*).[7]

These rules suggest the continuing relevance of E. E. Schattschneider's observation that our policy system is marked by a "mobilization of bias." However (and in this regard we are suggesting a modification of Schattschneider's notion), it is sometimes possible to achieve significant change in the guise of incrementalism if the importance of a seemingly narrow issue is not recognized by key political actors. Continued success may be achieved by intensive organizational intervention, with the knowledge that no easy victories are likely.

Several social scientists have called attention to the need for "thinking small." The broader the goals of a social movement, the more central its focus, and the greater its threat to the status quo, the less likely it is to succeed.[8] Single-issue reform-

---

[6] Raymond Bauer, Lewis A. Dexter, and Ithiel de Sola Pool, *Business and Public Policy* (New York: Atherton, 1963) as noted by Michael T. Hayes, "The Semi-Sovereign Pressure Groups," *Journal of Politics* 40 (Feb. 1978), 135.

[7] Murray Edelman, *Politics as Symbolic Action* (Chicago: Markham, 1971), ch. 1.

[8] Roberta Ash, *Social Movements in America* (Chicago: Markham, 1972), 29.

ist politics that does not threaten displacement of existing power configurations, then, may often provide the easiest route to success for emergent groups. Feminists have been reformist in focus, distinctly nonradical in method, and have tended to deal with each issue as discrete and separable from others, conforming to the above hypotheses. Correspondingly, the broader the goal sought and the more visible the issue, the more prevailing values are likely to be perceived as threatened and countermovements to form in intense opposition to change. Thus narrower *role equity* issues are most likely to produce success while *role change* issues often lead to intense, and not always resolvable, political conflict. As has been the experience for blacks in the political process, it may be that even the feminist thrust for equity is sometimes perceived as broadly redistributive of traditional values and resources. This has the potential for producing conflict with those people who wish to maintain existing power relationships.[9]

Using the distinction between role change and role equity explained above, we may say that the issue of equal credit opportunity conformed more closely to the role equity construct than the other three issues. Pregnancy disability was a role equity issue that generated divisiveness on the question of coverage for abortions. Title IX was a role equity issue that became controversial as aspects of the law and its regulations were perceived as affecting role change. Finally, abortion is an issue perceived as having profound implications for role change. Thus, of the issues examined in this volume, it has engendered the most controversy. In addition to this difference between role equity and role change, other factors sometimes influence opposition to feminist interests.[10] There is, for example, strong moral and religious opposition to abortion. Issues that are perceived as influencing role change have been

[9] See Harlan Hahn and Timothy Almy, "Ethnic Politics and Racial Issues," *Western Political Quarterly* 33 (Dec. 1971), 728.

[10] Hayes has distinguished between consensual and conflictual demand patterns, stressing the importance of political opposition ("The Semi-Sovereign Pressure Groups," 142).

more likely to produce united opposition than have issues seen to involve role equity. The feminist movement has been able to effectively neutralize opposition on the equity issues.

On three of the issues examined here—credit, pregnancy disability, and education—women have been able to provide a relatively united front despite some differences in opinion on specific tactics. However, on the abortion issue, women (although not the feminist movement) have been divided among themselves. Furthermore, when a group is able to manipulate the symbols of politics, it is in a position to help define the limits of debate.[11] In the case of changes in the credit law, women's groups were able to invoke the symbol of equal economic opportunity. On abortion there has been a continuing struggle over which political symbol will prevail—individual freedom or murder.

Contrary to the experience of public interest groups, the sometime allies of feminists for whom expansion of conflict has brought considerable success,[12] feminists have achieved most when they stressed the technical nature of an issue and sought to contain conflict within clear bounds. An example may be seen in the politics of the Equal Rights Amendment. In Congress, where the ERA succeeded in 1972 with broad majority support, the amendment was perceived as a legal issue and was discussed in abstract and technical terms. In the ratification process, where the ERA has faltered, the issues dealt with have become broader and the process came to highlight ideological values regarding society and change. Thus the presence of conflict has represented a bias against the adoption of any new policy: once conflict arises, differing views are presented; decision makers seek to avoid taking action; the politics of expediency can no longer prevail; and potential coalition partners will choose to stay aloof. Put in somewhat different terms, the group that succeeds in defining

[11] Edelman, *Politics as Symbolic Action*, ch. 2.

[12] Mark Nadel, *The Politics of Consumer Protection* (Indianapolis: Bobbs-Merrill, 1971), 160-205.

and limiting the parameters of debate may have a headstart on victory.

PLAN OF THE BOOK

In the next chapter there is a discussion of the mobilization of the contemporary women's movement and its evolution over the past decade. Chapter 3 considers the organization, funding, and strategies employed by feminist advocates. In the remainder of the book the four policy issues selected for analysis are examined. Finally, in the last chapter an assessment of the movement in relation to the policies studied is provided.

CHAPTER 2

FEMINIST MOBILIZATION

INTRODUCTION

Feminism lay dormant during the fifty-year period following the passage of the Nineteenth Amendment. The "new wave" of feminist groups is a product of the 1960s and 1970s. The contemporary feminist movement arose in a climate of social reform during a time when gaps between expectations and reality became more apparent. Technological advances and changes in societal values and lifestyles, together with changed consciousness, fostered development of the movement and finally the formation of formal group organizations.

The feminist groups that emerged as a social movement in the late 1960s and early 1970s evolved in the later years of the 1970s into a stage of political development that emphasized interest-group organization and professionalization. It must be remembered that feminist groups, despite their relatively broad support, have small formal memberships and have relied upon traditional women's organizations and a public generally supportive of equal rights for a constituency base. Feminists may benefit from decision makers' knowledge of increasingly widespread support for the basic principles of equal rights feminism. The 1980 Virginia Slims Poll found a large majority of women (64 percent) favoring efforts to change and strengthen the status of women, in contrast to a minority (40 percent) in 1970. A University of Michigan study found that support exceeds opposition for an equal role for women, for the women's rights movement, and for ratification of the

ERA. Women in voluntary traditional women's groups and local civic associations that are nonfeminist often demonstrate receptivity to women's rights issues, as long as they are related to equal rights and are presented in terms that do not threaten traditional lifestyles.[1] This point will be considered in greater detail in Chapter 3.

In the pages that follow, we will discuss the stages in the development of feminist groups—specifically, the social, political, and economic factors leading to group consciousness, the process of group mobilization, and the structure of groups.

THEORIES OF GROUP ORIGINS

The feminist groups that evolved in the past twenty years have tended to be leadership and not membership based, although both the National Organization for Women (NOW) and the National Abortion Rights Action League (NARAL) are exceptions to this generalization. Thus, even where some of the constructs we are about to review seem relevant to an understanding of the contemporary feminist movement, these theoretical frameworks provide only partial explanations for their development.

David Truman, in *The Governmental Process*, provides some general insight into the development of groups in American politics when he calls attention to the "phenomenon of organization in waves," suggesting that the formation of some groups may give rise to other groups.[2] Hence it can be sug-

[1] *1980 Virginia Slims American Women's Opinion Poll* (New York: Roper, 1980); Debrah Bokowski and Aage Clausen, "Federalism, Representation and the Amendment Process: The Case of ERA" (paper presented at the Midwest Political Science Association convention, Chicago, Ill., April 1979), 5; Susan Gluck Mezey and Trudy Haffron Bers, "Support for Women's Issues Among Local Civic Leaders" (paper presented at the American Political Science Association convention, Washington, D.C., Sept. 1, 1979), 6-14.

[2] David Truman, *The Governmental Process* (New York: Knopf, 1951), 60. For a more complete discussion of Truman's "disturbance" theory, see Jeffrey M. Berry, *Lobbying for the People* (Princeton: Princeton University Press, 1977), 19.

gested that the increased activities of the black civil rights movement influenced the mobilization of feminists.

William Chafe illuminates the emergence of the feminist movement in particular by attributing it to a point of view around which to organize, a positive response by a portion of the aggrieved group, and a conducive social atmosphere.[3] Charles Tilly has similarly contended that collective action involves recognition of a common interest, mobilization or control of resources (which provide the capacity to act on interests), and opportunity. A movement's formation and growth require an experience of events common to many people, strong emotional feelings of dissatisfaction, focus upon an outside object, and leadership.[4] The contemporary women's movement did in fact evolve in such a manner. No one event precipitated its mobilization. Rather, a convergence of conditions over time created an environment that was amenable to the reemergence of feminism.

Students of feminist politics like Jo Freeman have argued that when a movement emerges, it must rest on a preexisting communications network or infrastructure—like-minded people whose background, experience, or location will make them receptive to a new movement.[5]

Once a social movement has appeared, it may develop components of interest-group action. Interest-group organization reinforces leadership, communications, and incentives to participation.

The importance of leadership in the mobilization of previously unorganized interests is highlighted by Robert Salisbury, whose analysis of interest-group origins identifies en-

[3] William Chafe, *The American Woman: Her Changing Social, Economic and Political Roles, 1920-1970* (New York: Oxford University Press, 1972), 227.

[4] Charles Tilly, *From Mobilization to Revolution* (New York: Addison Wesley, 1978), 7.

[5] Jo Freeman, "Origins of the Women's Liberation Movement," in Joan Huber, ed., *Changing Women in a Changing Society* (Chicago: University of Chicago Press, 1973), 32.

trepreneurial dominance as the major precondition for group development.[6] In the early years of the feminist movement, such figures as Betty Friedan provided a focus for both communication and development of leadership. Salisbury, in his article on "An Exchange Theory of Interest Groups," suggests that "interest group origins, growth, death and associated lobbying activity may all be better explained if we regard them as exchange relationships between entrepreneur/organizers, who invest capital in a set of benefits, which they offer to prospective members at a price—membership."[7] Accordingly, his theory posits that individuals join groups because they derive benefits from participation.

The nature of incentives for individuals' involvement in groups has been the subject of much analysis. Peter Clark and James Q. Wilson identify three kinds—purposive, solidary, and material. Purposive incentives are ideologically based, solidary are socially rooted, and material are related to tangible rewards.[8] Mancur Olson further refines the notion of incentives for group membership by arguing that it is possible to organize latent support for groups only through the provision of selective incentives—nonpolitical positive inducements available only to group members.[9] Terry Moe has modified Olson's framework by suggesting that "purposive benefits can operate as selective incentives. . . . The support and pursuit of worthwhile collective goods" may provide sufficient rewards to some participants.[10] This notion of "in-process" benefits helps explain the nature of participation in feminist interest groups. "The individual will gain certain benefits from the process of participation itself, regardless of the outcome

[6] Robert Salisbury, "An Exchange Theory of Interest Groups," *Midwest Journal of Political Science* 13 (Feb. 1969), 1-32.

[7] *Ibid.*, 2.

[8] Peter B. Clark and James Q. Wilson, "Incentive Systems: A Theory of Organizations," *Administrative Science Quarterly* 6 (Sept. 1961), 129-66.

[9] Mancur Olson, *The Logic of Collective Action* (Cambridge, Mass.: Harvard University Press, 1971), 132-33.

[10] Terry Moe, "A Broader View of Interest Groups," *Journal of Politics* 43 (May 1981), 536.

of the process, . . . [and] these in-process benefits will outweigh [the] costs of contribution."[11] In the period during which the women's movement reemerged and developed an intricate network of policy-related interest groups, it is clear that incentives for participation were primarily of the "in-process" kind, and the societal conditions outlined by social movement theorists help account for group development and mobilization.

GENESIS OF THE MOVEMENT

As suggested above, the women's movement appears to have originated in changed social conditions. Without giving equal weight to all the factors cited below, we can say that there were several causes for the reemergence of feminism. Among these causes were socio-political conditions and technological innovations that served to transform the role of women as mothers and homemakers, albeit gradually over time. The latter included advances in medical science, especially contraception, which lowered the birthrate and consequently the time devoted to childrearing, and laborsaving devices that freed women from housework so that they had more time to perform other tasks. In the two decades from 1950 to 1970, moreover, female labor force participation almost doubled, reaching 40 percent by the end of the sixties.[12] These trends and others helped reinforce an environment of changing lifestyles, later marriage, more frequent divorce, greater sexual freedom, and the changed (if not diminished) role of the family, providing a favorable context for the resurgence of feminism.

In the 1960s a prevalent atmosphere of social reform contributed to the conditions that fostered feminist mobilization. One avenue into the feminist movement was participation in the civil rights and new left movements where, despite their

[11] Allen Buchanan, "Revolutionary Motivation and Rationality," *Philosophy & Public Affairs* 9 (Fall 1979), 68.

[12] Marcia Lee, "The Equal Rights Amendment," in David Caputo, ed., *The Politics of Policy Making in America* (San Francisco: W. H. Freeman, 1977), 16-17.

rhetoric of equality, women were relegated to subordinate roles and feminist interests were both neglected and scorned. This experience "radicalized" some women and led them to organize a variety of newer groups—*women's liberation groups*—that stressed, along with other concerns, "consciousness-raising," reflecting the shared experiences and discrimination suffered by women, and "alternative structures" such as self-help clinics and day-care centers. Many of these feminist activists began to question the validity of existing societal modes. From such women there emerged the more radical segment of the women's movement, which emphasized non-hierarchical, democratic, virtually leaderless (anti-) structures.

There were stark discrepancies between expectation and reality for educated middle-class women in the 1950s and 1960s. These women grew up encountering numerous contradictions in their lives; in particular, achievement-oriented values were incompatible with the traditional feminine role. In 1963 Betty Friedan wrote *The Feminine Mystique* describing the plight of overeducated women who were consigned to the role of homemakers and mothers. Her work was followed by that of Kate Millett, Germaine Greer, and others. The awareness aroused by these books, along with the model of tactical action and concern with oppression provoked by the civil rights and new left movements, was reinforced by the experiences of many women activists with the state commissions on the status of women, which brought together older middle-class women. The commissions produced considerable evidence that legal inequality existed for women, creating the expectation that change would occur. At the Third National Conference of State Commissions held in 1966 feminists were rebuffed by conference organizers who prevented them from submitting a formal motion that would have had the effect of urging government implementation of legislation forbidding sex discrimination.[13] This disappointment provided a major catalyst for the development of the *women's*

[13] This account is presented in Maren Lockwood Carden, *The New Feminist Movement* (New York: Russell Sage, 1974), 103-104.

rights movement. This movement was reformist, and its adherents were concerned with altering the status quo by using the traditional tools of American politics. After the meeting, in protest against the limitations on action or dissent, feminists came together to create the National Organization for Women. Other organizational mobilization of rights groups soon followed: the Women's Equity Action League (WEAL) was founded in 1968 and the National Women's Political Caucus (NWPC) in 1971.[14]

By the early 1970s the women's rights groups that emerged in the 1960s, as well as older and more traditional women's groups such as the League of Women Voters (LWV), American Association of University Women (AAUW), Business and Professional Women (BPW), and the General Federation of Women's Clubs (GFWC), were involved in a sophisticated endeavor, dividing responsibility for political activities and gaining congressional passage of the Equal Rights Amendment. The movement for the enactment of the ERA created policy networks—friendships, overlapping group memberships, and the like—which comprised the basis for renewed efforts in other policy areas. Mutual problem-solving, sharing of information, division of labor, efforts at creating coalition and unity, mobilization and recruitment of activists, and the gaining of positive access to media and government—all of which were to be built upon in future political efforts—emerged.

In addition, the relationship between women's liberation and women's rights groups began to change. By the late 1970s there was no longer a sharp distinction that could be drawn between women's rights and women's liberation groups.[15] Many of the ideas once held only by "liberation" advocates were now espoused by most feminists.

The liberation groups had adhered to strong principles based on anti-authoritarianism, participatory democracy, and uto-

14 Lee, "The Equal Rights Amendment," 16.

15 Maren Lockwood Carden, *Feminism in the Mid-1970's* (New York: Ford Foundation, 1977), 6.

pian communalism.[16] Sara Evans and Jo Freeman observed that the anti-leadership consensus adhered to by these groups proved inadequate as a basis for organization. "A preoccupation with internal processes . . . took precedence over program or effectiveness. As a result, women's liberation groups tended to oscillate between total formlessness at one extreme or a kind of collective authoritarianism on the other."[17] Among women's liberation groups, those women who developed an ability for public leadership received harsh criticism for being "stars." However, despite difficulties, a considerable portion of the more militant branch of feminism survived by joining with the mainstream of the movement. Other liberation groups began to organize numerous activities in communities throughout the nation. Liberation groups continue to exist in many local areas. These organizations publish myriad newspapers, magazines, and newsletters. They organize "Take Back the Night" marches to protest violence against women, speakouts on rape, consulting and support services for women (including bookstores), and such direct action efforts as shelters for battered women and child-care centers. Local feminists have organized collectives and have also developed caucuses and discussion groups within trade unions and professional organizations.

Much of the participatory ideology of early liberationists has remained an integral part of mainstream professional feminist politics. The relationship between liberation- and rights-oriented variants of feminism may be seen in the largest women's rights group, the National Organization for Women.[18] Although NOW remains a pragmatic and reformist group, it has altered some of its once more moderate mainstream po-

[16] See Wini Breines, "A Review Essay," *Feminist Studies*, Fall 1979, 502; also Joan Cassell, *A Group Called Women* (New York: McKay, 1977), 168.

[17] Sara Evans, *Personal Politics* (New York: Viking, 1980), 223. See also Jo Freeman, "The Tyranny of Structurelessness," in Jane Jaquette, ed., *Women in Politics* (New York: Wiley, 1974).

[18] Sheila Rothman, *Women's Proper Place* (New York: Basic Books, 1978), 245.

sitions.[19] For example, NOW and several other feminist groups have come to view the oppression of lesbians as an integral part of mainstream professional feminist politics, recognizing the right of individuals to determine their own sexuality and lifestyle. (Prior to 1970 lesbian rights were not part of NOW's program.) NOW has also increased its involvement in such broadly humanist areas of policy as prison reform and racial discrimination. In its earlier years it took no position on these issues.[20]

The current leaders of feminist groups might be termed "executive" rather than "charismatic"; their stress is not on concentrating their own power but on countering bureaucratic tendencies that place more and more people under control of a few. What Rosabeth Kanter has defined as "flattening hierarchy"—spreading authority and gaining greater participation—seems to be the prevalent mode in feminist groups, although it is difficult to generalize for all those groups discussed here.[21] As Maren Lockwood Carden wrote with reference to NOW: "Although NOW has moved steadily in the direction of greater institutionalization, . . . its members remain self-consciously determined to avoid becoming an impersonal bureaucratic organization and intend to combine the goal of organizational effectiveness with the goal of concern for the individual participant."[22]

Although feminist leaders (such as Betty Friedan and Gloria Steinem) were instrumental in the mobilization of a feminist movement that had remained dormant from the early 1920s to the mid-1960s, the ideology of the movement itself seems to have led over time to a modification of leadership roles for the contemporary movement. Most feminist leaders are well known within the movement but have little media visibility or public recognition. While individual leaders who had great

[19] *Ibid.*

[20] Carden, *The New Feminist Movement*, 117.

[21] Rosabeth Moss Kanter, *Men and Women of the Corporation* (New York: Basic Books, 1977), 276.

[22] Carden, *The New Feminist Movement*, 131.

determination and skill were largely responsible for the formation and early development of these groups, no feminist organization could echo these words used to describe Common Cause: "[John] Gardner's influence permeates the entire structure of Common Cause. It is hard for the staff of Common Cause to imagine their organization without Gardner, and thus when he hinted publicly that he might retire . . . many were genuinely shocked." Nor is there a feminist counterpart to Ralph Nader, of whom it has been written: "the ascetic, dedicated prophet of the public interest is the object of widespread admiration. Thousands of young people seek to emulate him."[23] The absence of personalized leadership among feminists may be attributable in part to movement ideology, which inspires women to be autonomous, take responsibility, make decisions, and develop their own positions. Group staffs are committed less to a specific leader than to the "movement" and its goals. Another factor mitigating against personalized leadership may be the early ideology that stressed "sisterhood," implying decentralization, internal democracy, nonhierarchical control, and the like. Although no longer dominant among such groups as NOW, whose "sisterhood" does not extend to total intraorganizational equality, there is still a prevailing belief in maximizing participation by the rank and file.[24] NOW builds in leadership change by holding biennial elections for new national leaders, a reflection of the desire to prevent domination by a single person or small elite. It seems evident that this commitment to avoidance of domineering leadership, and decision making through compromise and participation, is directly attributable to the ties of the movement to earlier liberation politics.

Organized feminism, though professionalized, has not lost

[23] Andrew McFarland, *Public Interest Lobbies* (Washington, D.C.: American Enterprise Institute, 1976), 20-21.

[24] Jo Freeman, "Resource Mobilization and Strategy: A Model for Analyzing Social Movement Organization Action" in Meyer Zald and John D. McCarthy, eds., *The Dynamics of Social Movements* (Cambridge, Mass.: Winthrop, 1979), 178.

its spontaneity and commitment—new elements continually join and renew organizational vigor, although groups themselves (including NOW) have become more hierarchical in structure and traditional in established procedures. The experience of NOW and other feminist groups seems thus to refute the view of Weber and Michels that bureaucratization and accommodation replace a movement's initial momentum. That model suggests that as an organization gains societal acceptance, it becomes bureaucratized and accommodates to society. Bureaucrats develop a vested interest in maintaining their organizational position and, in order to maintain their primacy, lead their organization toward conservatism and oligarchy. The desire for organizational maintenance, even at the expense of achievement of movement goals, becomes paramount, and the wish to avoid conflict becomes overriding.[25] Yet, as Zald and Ash have pointed out, this need not be the only fate of groups oriented to change.[26] The organizations in the contemporary women's movement have not fallen prey to the perils of bureaucratization. They have remained agents for change in the status of women in society even as they have worked to broaden understanding for the goals of the movement.

THE STRUCTURE AND TYPES
OF CONTEMPORARY FEMINIST GROUPS

Virtually all the women's groups discussed in this study have a traditional bureaucratic organizational structure. In addition, some have chapters or branches and a dues-paying membership. All of the groups have operating rules or by-laws and a prescribed governing system. Usually governance consists of a board (comprised of professionals, business persons, and

[25] Max Weber, *The Theory of Social and Economic Organization* (New York: Oxford University Press, 1947), 363-86; Robert Michels, *Political Parties* (New York: Dover, 1959), 370-73.

[26] Mayer Zald and Roberta Ash, "Social Movement Organizations: Growth, Decay, and Change," *Social Forces* 421 (1966), 327-40.

often leading group activists) that plays a role in raising money and in determining priorities and strategies. There is substantial overlap among board members within the feminist community. Most boards set broad policy but do not interfere in day-to-day staff activities. An exception is the Reproductive Freedom Project of the American Civil Liberties Union where board and staff functions are blurred among the eight attorneys who share joint concerns and consult frequently. Several feminist groups (WEAL and NOW-LDEF) have developed professionally from once largely voluntary organizations, have built stronger staffs in recent years, and have emerged from an era of board dominance. Most of the groups began as leadership or cadre organizations lacking a mass base. Some, such as NARAL and NOW, have developed constituencies while still others (WLDF, for one) would like to. Some, such as WEAL, prefer to exist with a small membership.

Although groups have become bureaucratized, they have not tended to rigidify or become more conservative. Rather, they have reinforced and even expanded their initial range and activities while sustaining or deepening their commitment to social change, albeit incremental in scope.

The growth and development of feminist groups were aided by the existence of traditional women's voluntary groups such as the American Association of University Women, National Council of Jewish Women, and League of Women Voters. Feminist political consciousness and mobilization were heightened by the struggle for congressional ratification of the ERA, which helped create a network of contacts, communication, mutual problem-solving, and information-sharing. Feminist groups proliferated in the 1970s so that the initial movement spearheaded by NOW diversified with groups specializing in litigation, research, policy formulation and analysis, and constituency development—though some groups participate in more than one activity.

Like their earlier black civil rights counterparts, feminist groups are frequently based in Washington or New York. By 1973 many of the groups including the (now defunct) Women's Lobby, WEAL, NOW, and NWPC had opened Washington offices in order specifically to influence the national policy process.

The groups whose roles will be considered in this chapter include the Women's Rights Project (WRP) and Reproductive Freedom Project (RFP) of the American Civil Liberties Union (ACLU), Women's Rights Project of the Center for Law and Social Policy (CLASP), the National Organization for Women (NOW) and its affiliates, the NOW Legal Defense and Education Fund (NOW-LDEF) and the NOW Project on Equal Education Rights (PEER), Women's Equity Action League (WEAL) and the WEAL Fund, Women's Legal Defense Fund (WLDF), National Women's Political Caucus (NWPC), Center for Women Policy Studies (CWPS), and National Abortion Rights Action League (NARAL).

These groups can be divided into four different types. Together they have created a network of complementary alliances in national politics, despite the existence of potential strains that exist owing to the presence of their often disparate constituencies.

It should be noted that several groups maintain different arms, each with a different tax status and different purpose. For example, NOW with 501(c)(4) status—which means that while the organization is tax-exempt, contributions to it are not tax-deductible—has established a Legal Defense and Education Fund that has a 501(c)(3) tax status; contributions are tax-deductible, but the organization is limited as to the time it can expend in lobbying activity. NOW has also established a Political Action Committee (PAC) to engage in campaign-related activities.

The four types of groups that comprise the national feminist political community are *mass-based* or *membership* feminist organizations such as NOW and NWPC; *specialized* feminist groups, including litigation and research groups, which often provide the technical expertise and legal acumen that have led to feminist successes in the administrative, legislative, and judicial arenas; *single-issue* groups such as NARAL, AIAW

26

(Association for Intercollegiate Athletics for Women), PEER (which monitors Title IX in education), and SPRINT (a WEAL Fund affiliate concerned with equal athletic opportunity); and *traditional* women's groups, which support many but not all feminist goals (for example, some are avowedly "pro-choice" and some are not) and whose support of these goals is not the major objective or function of the group. Political efforts by feminists have been facilitated on numerous occasions because of the mass constituency base and contacts maintained by these more established women's groups (see Tables 1 and 2).

The newest component, and potentially a fifth set, of groups in feminist politics is an *electoral campaign sector*, which developed in the late 1970s and gained additional momentum prior to the 1980 election campaign. In addition to the political action committees (PACs) established by the NWPC, NOW, and NARAL in accordance with new campaign finance regulations, autonomous groups such as Voters for Choice now seek to "target" legislators opposed to abortion. They have borrowed this technique from the efforts portrayed as successful by the media in which anti-feminist groups have

TABLE 1
Membership of
Traditional Women's Groups (1980)

American Association of University Women	190,000
B'nai Brith Women	120,000
League of Women Voters	115,000
General Federation of Women's Clubs	600,000
National Federation of Business and Professional Women's Clubs	154,000
National Council of Jewish Women	100,000
United Methodist Women	1,244,000
	Total 2,523,000

SOURCE: Telephone survey, July 15, 1981.

TABLE 2
Feminist Groups' Membership and
Staff Resources (1978)

Group	Membership	Professional Staff
ACLU-WRP/RFP	none	12*
CLASP-WRP	none	3
CWPS	none	10
NARAL	90,000†	18 (includes interns and volunteers)
NOW	125,000	30
NOW-LDEF	none	16‡
NWPC	50,000	8 (plus 4 part-time)
WEAL	3,500	21§
WLDF	800	15

SOURCE: Annual reports of the groups and personal interviews.

* Including Richmond office and Washington lobbyist whose work addresses race- and sex-related issues.

† 1980 membership data.

‡ Including PEER and LDEF's Michigan Project that employs additional staff.

§ Including WEAL, WEAL Fund, and SPRINT.

used the electoral system to pursue their goals. The campaign-oriented groups rely extensively on direct mail in order to raise money. These efforts mark a new stage in feminist political development. In addition, the Women's Campaign Fund provides resources for female candidates seeking electoral office who have a commitment to women's rights. Support for ERA (and not necessarily "pro-choice" views), for example, has qualified prospective recipients for backing by the group.[27]

[27] In addition to the groups we examine in the text, we also interviewed attorneys from the League of Women Voters (Maureen Thornton) and the Women's Law Fund (Jane Picker) as well as directors of Voters for Choice

Feminist Membership Groups

Among the earliest feminist groups to develop were the National Organization for Women and the National Women's Political Caucus. Although these organizations are membership organizations, they lack the mass constituency of such traditional women's groups as the General Federation of Women's Clubs (cf. Tables 1 and 2). NOW is patterned (though perhaps not consciously) after the National Association for the Advancement of Colored People (NAACP). Following the NAACP model, NOW has developed different components in order to maximize fund-raising and flexibility. In addition to the mass-membership-based NOW organization, a NOW Legal Defense and Education Fund was established, as well as PEER to emphasize monitoring of Title IX enforcement and a PAC to stress ballot-box reprisals against recalcitrant legislators.

NOW increased its membership from 1,122 and 14 chapters in 1967 to 125,000 members and 700 chapters in each of the fifty states in 1978, largely owing to its campaign for ERA ratification. Members receive the group's publication, *National NOW Times*. Local chapters are autonomous. In contrast to the NAACP and Urban League, which derive significant revenue from local affiliates and branches, NOW rebates 4 percent of its revenue to state chapters.

NOW is the largest feminist constituency group. It has an unusually strong board, which is elected by regional representatives on a biennial basis, and five national officers, who are selected at a national convention. The two-year-term national officers, who manage the Washington offices, are salaried by the organization. In a somewhat unusual organizational structure, these officers are involved in the daily operations of the organization as well as in decision making. A thirty-

and Women's Campaign Fund. Because of space constraints, their comments are not analyzed in depth, but some of their insights are included. One other group, the Women's Lobby, under the direction (and considerable financial support) of Carole Burris, has been the feminist movement's first casualty.

person staff includes ten field operatives, researchers, organizers, lobbyists, and specialists in specific areas such as reproductive freedom, lesbian rights, and economic rights. They all operate under the direction of national officers. (NOW's Legal Defense and Education Fund and the Project for Equal Education Rights will be discussed below in the section on research and litigation groups.)

During its history NOW has been beset by attacks internally from both the right and the left: members who have opposed its current and past advocacy of abortion rights and sexual self-determination, and members who oppose NOW's reformist, pragmatic approach to changing the existing political system, respectively. Nonetheless, it has weathered internal conflicts such as these as well as those engendered by creation of and communication with local chapters.[28]

NOW and other feminist groups have experienced major changes in leadership and organization since their formation but have sustained and strengthened their political role. NOW's 1967 Bill of Rights still remains a guide to the general demands of the feminist movement:

1. an equal rights constitutional amendment;
2. enforcement of laws banning sex-based employment discrimination;
3. maternity leave rights in employment and social security benefits;
4. tax deductions for child and home care expenses for working parents;
5. child-care centers;
6. equal and unsegregated education;
7. equal job training opportunities and allowances for women in poverty;
8. the right of women to control their reproductive lives.[29]

Another constituency organization in the women's movement is the National Women's Political Caucus, which ex-

[28] Carden, *The New Feminist Movement*, 103-18.
[29] Barbara Deckard, *The Women's Movement* (New York: Harper and Row, 1979), 348.

panded its membership from 271 members in 1971 to 50,000 in 1978. Most "members," however, are merely "associates" or contributors rather than active group participants; "governing" members number 11,000 and play a more participatory role in the organization. The NWPC publishes a newsletter, *Women's Political Times*. It is governed by a steering committee comprised of state and local caucus representatives. The staff includes eight professionals and several seasonal consultants. The NWPC focuses on electing women as national convention delegates and on electing women to public office. Hence, while the caucus does lobby and is active in Washington-based coalitions, its primary orientation is the electoral process and, in recent years, the ratification of the ERA as well.

Like NWPC, the Women's Equity Action League has a membership base but is not primarily a membership organization. WEAL was founded in Ohio in 1968 as a reaction to what was then perceived as NOW's radical stand on abortion and in an effort to provide "respectability" to the feminist movement. In 1972 its tax-exempt arm, the WEAL Fund, was established largely to support lawsuits and to monitor implementation and enforcement; it has focused on Title IX and academic discrimination. The WEAL Fund now plays the dominant role in staff and funding within the WEAL organizational structure and also operates SPRINT, a clearinghouse on women in athletics. WEAL and the WEAL Fund have interlocking directorates but separate staffs. The board of the WEAL Fund, which includes five attorneys, maintained a dominant role in that organization until the late 1970s. But the board's role has been modified as the once largely voluntary structure has been altered and a paid professional staff has developed. The membership of WEAL itself has not expanded since its establishment; in 1978 it was 3,500. WEAL's primary constituency of professional and executive women has sought to mobilize expertise rather than numbers.[30]

[30] Freeman, "Resource Mobilization and Strategy," 185.

Specialized Groups

The growth of WEAL and the WEAL Fund from a small office operation to an organization with a staff of twenty-one employees in 1978 is paralleled by the growth of the Center for Women Policy Studies, a small nonmembership organization founded in 1972 to provide technical expertise on various women's issues. In 1978 it had a staff of ten professionals, and though it has lost one of its founders and co-directors, the CWPS continues to expand. The scope of the organization's issue concerns ranges from equal credit to battered women. The board of three (consisting of the director, former co-director, and academician Jessie Bernard) plays a strong role. The Center has published numerous scholarly works documenting economic discrimination as well as other systematic discrimination against women.

In addition, there are several groups with litigational focuses, though not necessarily extensive litigational capacity,[31] whose strategy is to become involved in precedent-setting cases, much like their civil rights predecessors. However, there is no one dominant feminist legal group comparable to the NAACP Legal Defense and Educational Fund for civil rights groups. This is the result of several factors, including foundations' funding practices that have encouraged a multiplicity of groups, the role of several strong personalities who have led to multiple organizational growth, and specialization by issue-specific organizations.

Thus several groups, each with three or four attorneys plus support staff, coexist. In this respect, they resemble the small-scale operations of the NAACP and ACLU in their formative stages from 1940 to 1960.[32] Many litigation groups do far more than just case law, and they increasingly devote their time to other tasks. The executive director of one such group

---

[31] Several feminist law firms exist outside the Washington/New York axis; they include the Women's Law Fund in Cleveland and Equal Rights Advocates in California. They are not being considered here.

[32] Robert Rabin, "Lawyers for Social Change: Perspectives on Public Interest Law," *Stanford Law Review* 28 (Jan. 1976), 213.

operates as a "linkage" person among feminist interests and among civil rights groups coordinating, bringing them together, sharing information, and "politicking." She spends relatively little time actually litigating.

The Center for Law and Social Policy began in 1969 as a public interest law firm, initiated its women's rights project in 1974, and now employs three attorneys on this project. Its advisory board is predominantly local (Washington-based), and its Litigation Committee serves to advise on the broad nature of cases to be dealt with. The Center's lawyers have been particularly active on Title IX and on health issues as they relate to women. One observer has remarked that the Center functions as a law firm for women's organizations that do not yet have the skills or resources necessary to support litigation. It has developed expertise in analyzing government regulations and securing their enforcement.

The American Civil Liberties Union has given rise to two feminist-oriented litigation groups. The first was the Women's Rights Project, an outgrowth of the 1971 Supreme Court case *Reed* v. *Reed*,[33] which provided the ACLU with the idea that the equal protection clause might have potential as a vehicle to increase rights for women. With the aid of Ford Foundation funding and matching grants from other foundations, the project began in New York City. Four attorneys now work on the Women's Rights Project. The project also operates an office (of nonlawyers) in Richmond, Virginia, which functions primarily as a force for community organizing and public education on women's rights. (The ACLU office in Washington employs a full-time lobbyist on women's and other rights issues, funded by the ACLU itself.)

In 1974, prompted in part by the reluctance of contributors (primarily the Ford Foundation) to support abortion-related cases and in part by the concentration of the Women's Rights Project leadership on other areas, the Reproductive Freedom

[33] 404 U.S. 71.

Project was founded by the ACLU with the aid of funding from John D. Rockefeller III. Monthly meetings between the staff and a four-person advisory committee (all feminist attorneys) have come, by all accounts, closest of all groups examined to blurring distinctions between board and staff in function and expertise. The meetings are strategy sessions, which are supplemented by more frequent intraoffice consultations. Today the feminist legal staff of seven at the ACLU is the largest "group" in the organization, leading one writer to suggest that feminists have "coopted" the ACLU.[34] The RFP both litigates on abortion rights and functions as an informational resource center.

The growth and development of the Women's Legal Defense Fund, as well as NOW's Legal Defense and Education Fund, may be attributed to their directors. WLDF was founded in 1971 by a small group of well-known feminist lawyers in Washington, D.C., with the aid of a start-up grant from the Junior League. Originally a volunteer organization that borrowed from the model of the ACLU and the Lawyers Committee for Civil Rights under Law in obtaining *pro bono* private counsel, the Fund now employs fifteen people, including five attorneys. It still does no in-house litigation. Under the direction of Judith Lichtman, the Fund has grown from an organization with a $30,000 budget and 85 members to one that in 1978 had 800 members and a budget of $250,000.[35] WLDF is now seeking to expand its membership to 10,000 national dues-payers. The organization has a board of elected members and chairpersons of standing committees, most of whom are attorneys. A nine-person screening committee determines what cases the Fund should accept. Volunteers continue to play a key role in the organization's work, which alone among feminist groups discussed here operates a local service—a shelter for battered women.

NOW's Legal Defense and Education Fund is linked to its

[34] Freeman, "Resource Mobilization and Strategy," 175.
[35] WLDF, *Annual Report* (July 1978 – June 1979), 11.

parent organization NOW through an intricate corporate relationship. NOW-LDEF is governed by its own board (and by-laws) consisting of NOW officers, ten elected directors, and eight directors appointed by the board. At least five members of the board must be attorneys. A Defense Committee reviews participation in litigation. The Fund's headquarters are in New York while both national NOW and NOW-LDEF's offshoot PEER are located in Washington, D.C. Similar to the board of the WEAL Fund, NOW-LDEF's board is active and involved although no longer dominant, owing to the new role of the enlarged and strengthened staff. Like the NAACP Legal Defense and Educational Fund, whose model it has emulated, NOW-LDEF is seeking to develop a group of cooperating attorneys. Director Phyllis Segal inherited a litigation budget of $4,000 when she came to the Fund as its first full-time staff attorney in 1976, and it grew to $110,879 by 1979. By 1980 the staff had enlarged to include four attorneys, and the total budget was estimated to be $1.5 million. The major focus of NOW-LDEF is education and public information, not litigation.[36]

Single-Issue Groups

The National Abortion Rights Action League, a single-issue "pro-(abortion) choice" group, is an outgrowth of an earlier feminist organization that sought to repeal restrictive abortion laws at the state level. At that time it was known as the National Association to Repeal Abortion Laws. In 1973, in response to the Supreme Court decisions on abortion, and fearing a countermovement from the right, the group's name was changed and its headquarters moved from New York to Washington, D.C. NARAL is not only a feminist organization; it also has numerous ties to population and health groups. It has always counted among its members public health activists and medical professionals as well as feminists. Like NOW, WEAL, and several other civil rights groups, NARAL has

[36] NOW-LDEF, *1979 Annual Report*, 15.

several arms—one that lobbies, having 501(c)(4) status, a 501(c)(3) Foundation, and a PAC to engage in electoral campaign activity. NARAL, like NWPC and CWPS, has no litigation capacity, although it can contract legal work to be done. With a staff of eighteen and an active Executive Committee of fifteen (which meets every six weeks), NARAL, under pressure from right-to-life opposition, seems to be expanding its focus from being primarily a Washington-based group to developing grassroots organization as well. By the end of the 1970s it had grown from an organization of 20,000 to 90,000 members as a result of a direct-mail recruiting effort. The emergence of single-issue groups like NARAL has freed organizations like NOW to participate in more diverse causes.

NOW's Project on Equal Education Rights (PEER) was founded in 1974 to monitor enforcement of Title IX in Washington, D.C. Its nine-person staff has been supplemented by a new project in Michigan to initiate grassroots activity on Title IX through organizing, monitoring, and bringing complaints from the local level. PEER has its own (albeit inactive) advisory council.

CONCLUSION

Feminist organizations evolved as energetic interest-group actors in the 1960s and 1970s. Their development was based in large measure on changed societal relationships that fostered the generation of new demands on public policy makers. The women's movement has been able to integrate many divergent interests, by virtue of group proliferation and concern for inclusivity.

CHAPTER 3

THE GROUP ACTORS: RESOURCES AND STRATEGIES

INTRODUCTION

As Chapter 2 makes clear, the organized feminist movement has grown remarkably, in both the number of constituency groups and its political influence, since its relatively recent beginnings in the 1960s. Today it is poorer than its counterparts in the civil rights movement, having entered politics together with a large number of other competing "rights" groups. Group resources including staff, funding, and membership both dictate and constrain possibilities for political influence. Nonetheless, feminist groups have proliferated, and new and old groups alike have grown and become increasingly professionalized in the last several years. These groups come together regularly in numerous coalitions and exchanges, linked by intersecting sets of personal relationships and contacts. Feminists have been particularly effective in developing autonomous, specialized organizations while preserving the cohesiveness of the movement. Bound to the movement and its abstract ideology rather than to a specific leader or set of leaders, feminists have avoided rivalries based on personal loyalties.

Feminist groups examined here are reformist or "norm-oriented" in setting their goals.[1] Though their very existence

---

[1] Neil Smelser, *Theory of Collective Behavior* (New York: Free Press, 1963), 270-312.

represents a commitment to changing the social structure and the distribution of rewards within society, they reflect the scope and bias of the system. They are committed to gaining equal rights within existing society rather than creating a new society based on new values. In other words, they seek change in institutions instead of new institutions. Policy makers within the movement are trained professionals who are pragmatic, compromise-oriented individuals willing to settle for incremental change. They largely eschew expressive for more instrumental politics and deemphasize long-range planning and program development.

However, though there is an absence of overall "strategizing" and planning within the movement, it seems that the ad hoc nature of policy development is particularly well suited to constraints determined by the structure of the political system, a system characterized itself by incrementalism and shifting policy concerns. In the absence of ideological rigidity, flexibility may be maximized. It is possible, nevertheless, that some groups may find that they will need to define their own role and mission more precisely should they wish to maintain or augment membership and funding as well as gain greater rationality in resource allocation in the future.

Finally, the women's movement, like other reform movements, has had a problem recruiting and mobilizing latent constituencies, in whose name they gain credibility, owing to the "free rider" problem. Mancur Olson has pointed out that a group's ability to mobilize constituents may be severely limited when collective benefits or goods obtainable by group efforts accrue to group members whether or not they are active participants in the organization.[2] There is no material incentive for mass participation unless selective benefits or services are obtainable only by virtue of group membership. That feminist groups have been unable to develop such selective incentives (in contrast to the aged, for example, who may receive

[2] Mancur Olson, *A Theory of Collective Action* (Cambridge, Mass.: Harvard University Press, 1971), 48.

insurance and medical benefits with formal group membership) may provide a partial explanation for their failure to recruit more than a fraction of potential members. They are thus *responsive* but not *responsible* to a broad constituency base. Nonetheless, feminists may be in a stronger political position than membership figures only would indicate owing to their relationship with traditional women's groups on whose support and numbers they rely. In addition, as suggested above, these groups have the sympathy of countless men and women who adhere to many movement principles but do not hold formal membership in any organization.

GROUP RESOURCES

For feminist groups, organizational resources such as staff, finances, and membership tend to structure patterns of advocacy and impact. We will examine the resources available to feminist groups and then examine tactics and strategies for utilizing these resources in the political arena.

Staff

A major resource for all of the feminist groups examined in this study is their dedicated staff. Mancur Olson has hypothesized that individuals tend to join and maintain interest-group membership if they gain "separate and selective" incentives, normally of a nonpolitical nature, and when all access to those incentives is monopolized by the group. In the case of ideologically oriented interests, such as the women's movement, material incentives are not applicable. Terry Moe and Allen Buchanan have pointed out that the satisfaction of participating in a worthy cause may provide its own "selective incentives" for members of noneconomic groups.[3] In addition, incentives for staff and activist leaders may differ from those

[3] Allen Buchanan, "Revolutionary Motivation and Rationality," *Philosophy & Public Affairs* 9 (Fall 1979), 68; Terry Moe, "A Broader View of Interest Groups," *Journal of Politics* 43 (May 1981), 536-37.

attractive to members—an issue not discussed by Olson and other incentive theorists.

On the basis of the interviews conducted for this study, it is clear that most feminist group staff and leaders have made a conscious decision to place strictly economic rewards in a secondary position because of their basic concern for achieving social reform. Substantial numbers of female recruits join feminist organizations (often directly from law school or graduate school) because of a commitment to the particular cause, work with the feminist organizations for several years, and, when they do leave the groups, often remain in the public interest arena or join government agencies in areas where their training and movement identification are crucial.

Recruits to feminist activism tend to be well educated and middle class. Most of those interviewed were relatively young (under 50, many under 40), and many had law degrees or graduate degrees, primarily from good Eastern colleges or large public universities. They are predominantly attorneys. Salaries paid by feminist groups are clearly lower than those paid by the private sector and lower than those paid by government, with most in the range of $20,000 to $25,000 (see Table 3). Nonetheless, even accounting for inflation, they compare favorably to salaries paid public interest lobbyists as reported in a 1976 study.[4]

The incentives that motivate initial recruitment and willingness to remain are purposive (ideological) and solidary (social).[5] Individuals are drawn into the movement's network by ideology and often personal relationships, and they remain

---

[4] Joel Handler, Ellen Hollingsworth, and Howard Erlanger, *Lawyers and the Pursuit of Legal Rights* (New York: Academic Press, 1978), 85; and Jeffrey M. Berry, *Lobbying for the People* (Princeton: Princeton University Press, 1977), 102, Table IX-7.

[5] See Robert Salisbury, "An Exchange Theory of Interest Groups," *Midwest Journal of Political Science* 13 (Feb. 1969), 16. James Q. Wilson, in *Political Organizations* (New York: Basic Books, 1973), discusses incentive structures in a similar manner.

TABLE 3
Professional Salaries (1979)

ACLU	$23,000–30,000
CLASP-WRP	18,000–36,000
CWPS	26,000–35,000
NARAL	16,000–18,800
NOW	11,000–29,000
NOW-LDEF	14,000–31,000
NWPC	14,000–27,000
WEAL Fund	20,000
WLDF	18,000–26,500

SOURCE: Annual reports and personal interviews.

part of the complex organizational structure described below through extensive contacts, networks, and social ties.

One compensation for lack of economic rewards may be the access to power and even media publicity that participation in the movement can bring. Young women, even those with limited experience, may find themselves involved with exciting issues, talking with well-known politicians, and coming before the public in leadership roles. These rewards may provide a rationale for continued hard work, long hours, and low salaries.

Interviewees did complain of frustration in their work and spoke of a "burn-out" period—loosely estimated to be seven years—caused by delays, red tape, and other governmental foot-dragging as well as the never-ending nature of monitoring, necessary even after favorable legal decisions or acts of legislation have been achieved. Nonetheless, despite financial and psychological pressures and the inevitable turnover that results, a substantial number of leaders have remained with their groups.[6] It should be noted that, in addition to student

[6] Among those who have endured for a lengthy period are Marcia Greenberger and Margaret Kohn of CLASP-WRP, Jane Roberts Chapman of the CWPS, and Holly Knox of PEER.

interns, many groups (including the WEAL Fund and WLDF) supplement their regular work force through the use of volunteers, although increased professionalization is likely to limit the future role of volunteers since feminists are sensitive to the issue of "exploitation" without "compensation."

Although the focus of this study is not on internal decision-making processes within feminist groups, the importance of staff dominance in most groups should be noted. Increasingly, as feminist groups have emerged from an era of board dominance and reliance on volunteers, staffs have assumed leadership roles in selecting issues and employing tactics and strategies for political influence. In addition, as Jeffrey Berry suggests, a group's concentration on particular issues is also restricted by previous commitments and focus and by financial resources as well.[7] We now turn to the crucial matter of funding for feminist interest groups.

Funding

Sources of funding for women's movement groups are diverse, with membership and nonmembership contributions (especially from foundations), assistance from other groups, and government aid all providing some of the revenue. However, a 1976 study of public interest groups (which included many of the groups considered here) found that law centers serving racial and ethnic minorities were better funded than feminist groups. The latter had the smallest percentage of contributions as a proportion of their available revenues.[8] All the groups considered here have financial constraints, and almost all are dependent on contributions from outside funding sources whose impact may be to distort organizational goals and resource allocation. Many groups get grants or contracts from such diverse government agencies as the Equal Employment Opportunity Commission, Civil Rights Commission, Department

[7] Berry, *Lobbying for the People*, 203-205.
[8] The Council for Public Interest Law, *Balancing the Scales of Justice* (1975), 95 and 107.

of Labor, and the Department of State. For example, the WEAL Fund derives over half of its revenue from Women's Educational Equity Act (WEEA) funds channeled through the U.S. Office of Education (see Table 4). Reliance on government grants is viewed as a mixed blessing by most groups since it is seen as limiting freedom of action. Another hazard is that incoming administrators of government agencies may cut previously established ties and establish their own. Furthermore, acceptance of government funds may mute criticism of enforcement practices—a type of cooptation—though none of the group actors questioned on this issue thought that their own organization was limited in this manner. Nonetheless, one group referred to its "Byzantine relationship" with the Department of Health, Education, and Welfare; the group in question both receives funding from HEW and monitors sex discrimination laws under that Department's jurisdiction.

One source of funding for groups that have a public "image" is direct-mail soliciting of contributions from individuals. NOW-LDEF received $249,078 in individual contributions in 1978, almost triple what it received in 1976 owing to a massive mail campaign.[9] Direct mail also has helped NOW and NARAL increase their memberships. WLDF now utilizes this method as well. Direct mail thus seems to be a growing source of revenue for both membership and contributions, although it is costly in staff time and mailing expenses. Several groups have indicated that they tap individual contributors—men as well as women—several times annually. Increasingly, feminists may seek funds from women themselves as female workforce participation and income grow. A problem with reliance on individual funding may be its ephemeral nature; as economic conditions and popular issues change, such contributions may decrease.

Other sources of income include membership dues. For NOW and NARAL, for example, this comprises the major source of revenue. Many groups have several categories of paying

[9] NOW-LDEF, *Annual Report, 1976*, 18. It may benefit from public association with its parent organization, NOW.

TABLE 4
Major Sources of Revenue (1978)*

Group	Annual Budget	Funding Sources	Amount	% of Total
ACLU-WRP	$300,000	foundations		100
ACLU-RFP	156,000	foundations		100
CLASP-WRP	156,000	government		
		contracts	$3,000	2.6
		foundations	152,000	97.4
CWPS	209,476	government		
		contracts	206,476	98.6
NARAL	1,800,000	membership dues		
		and contributions	1,710,000	100
NOW	2,654,000†	membership dues	1,845,000	69.5
		individual		
		contributions	615,000	23.2
		sales	76,000	2.9
NOW-LDEF	602,828	foundations	287,929	47.8
		individual		
		contributions	249,078	41.3
		corporate		
		contributions	21,100	3.5
NWPC	750,000‡	individual		
		contributions	399,000	53.2
		fund-raising		
		events	266,000	35.5
WEAL Fund§	379,674	government		
		grants	108,251	28.5
		government		
		contracts	159,672	42.0
		foundations	73,269	19.3
WLDF	243,076	government		
		grants	53,907	22.2
		foundations	139,616	57.4

Table 4 (cont.)

SOURCE: All data derive from available annual reports and from *Comsearch Printouts, 1977-78, 1978-79* (New York: Foundation Center, 1978 and 1979), nos. 63, 64, 65, 88. Available information included 1978 audits or reports from NOW, NOW-LDEF, CWPS, NWPC, WEAL Fund, a letter from CLASP-WRP, and telephone interviews with Aryeh Neier and Ira Glasser, past and present directors of the ACLU, respectively.

* The totals in the last column will not always add up to 100 percent because we have included only major sources and not all sources of revenues for the groups.

† Only 1979 figures were available.

‡ Includes NWPC/ERA.

§ Includes Rawalt Legal Defense Fund.

members. One drawback is that membership often requires organizations to provide some sort of service, however limited, in the form of newsletters, periodicals, or the like, which may cost almost as much as the revenue that can be raised from dues.

Some litigation groups derive a portion of their funds (shifting as different cases are settled each year) from recoveries for attorney's fees. It should be noted that the Supreme Court's 1975 decision in *Alyeska Pipeline Service Co. v. Wilderness Society*[10] curtailed the award of attorneys' fees unless there is a specific statutory authorization for such an award. This has limited fee awards in many feminist cases that do not entail such authorization, except those relating to Title VII, which does authorize fee awards. However, groups that obtain *pro bono* legal services derive the equivalent of thousands of dollars annually in "free" legal time from cooperating attorneys.

A growing source of revenue for some groups, including NOW and NWPC, comes from charges for dinners and receptions. Selling pins, t-shirts, and posters, as well as magazine subscriptions and the use of advertising space in publications, is another new way of building revenue.

It should be noted that groups that are part of a larger organization (the WRP of the ACLU) receive in varying degrees valuable "in kind" services from their sponsoring organization. These services include access to telephones, ad-

[10] 421 U.S. 240.

ministrative help, and the like, which would require raising further revenue if they were not made available gratis.

Perhaps most significant, finally, is the role of foundations. In 1967 the Ford Foundation "made a major commitment to civil rights and disadvantaged minorities," listing four areas of action: community development, civil rights litigation, civil rights advocacy, and public interest law[11] (see Table 5). Only in a few instances have foundations other than Ford contributed more to any one feminist group's revenues, though the PEER project to monitor Title IX received $275,000 from Carnegie as part of its joint support arrangement with Ford. Major foundation contributors to feminist groups other than Ford include the Rockefeller Foundation, the Carnegie Corporation, Rockefeller Brothers Fund, the Field Foundation, and the Edna McConnell Clark Foundation. Kellogg, the New York Foundation, and others contribute in varying amounts to different groups. Several feminist groups have received small grants from the Playboy and Ms. Foundations. A grant from John D. Rockefeller III was instrumental in getting the Reproductive Freedom Project of the ACLU started; the Rock-

TABLE 5

Ford Foundation Grants (1978)

(grants generally made for two-year periods)

ACLU-WRP	$300,000
CLASP-WRP	280,000
NOW-LDEF	225,000
PEER (NOW-LDEF)	184,000
WEAL Fund	150,000
WLDF	104,000

SOURCE: *Comsearch Printouts, 1977-78, 1978-79* (New York: Foundation Center, 1978 and 1979), nos. 63, 64, 65, 88.

[11] Robert McKay, *Nine for Equality under Law: Civil Rights Litigation* (New York: Ford Foundation, 1977), 9.

efeller gift helped generate other contributions as well. It should be noted that, virtually alone among the groups studied here, the RFP receives no funds from Ford; in fact, its funding pattern is unusual because the Project draws small grants, generally under $50,000 and often under $20,000, from a number of different foundations.[12]

As a rule, established black civil rights groups receive far more substantial funding than feminist groups. According to figures provided by Susan Berresford of the Ford Foundation, Ford funding for all feminist groups (including educational institutions and programs as well as advocacy groups) from 1972 to 1979 averaged 2.1 percent of the total grants that were made (compared with 40 percent for black civil rights groups in 1970).[13] Numerous studies have documented the relatively impoverished state of feminist groups. In 1976 feminist litigation groups received only 3 percent of all foundation grants, and all of these women's groups had incomes of less than $300,000. Further evidence indicates that, from 1972 to 1974, $12 million of $2 billion in grants provided by foundations went to improve the status of women—less than one-fifth of 1 percent.[14] A 1979 study of funding of women's groups by the Ford Foundation included *none* of the groups examined here among the "top ten" women's group recipients cited. This study also reported that most feminist groups that are grant recipients receive only one grant from each foundation (whereas many black civil rights groups receive more than one grant).[15] Of six foundations that derive their assets primarily from sales of cosmetics to women, only 4.7 percent

[12] Telephone interviews with Aryeh Neier and Ira Glasser of the ACLU, Feb. 22, 1980.

[13] Telephone interview with Susan Berresford, Program Officer, Ford Foundation, Jan. 1980.

[14] Mary Jean Tully, "Funding the Feminists," *Foundation News* (March/April 1975), 26.

[15] *Financial Support of Women's Programs in the 1970's* (New York: Ford Foundation, July 1979), 7.

(of \$26 million) of their grant awards went to women's pro-grams in 1975-76.[16] The only cosmetics-based foundation providing significant support for women's groups is the Helena Rubenstein Foundation.

Why have feminist groups been disadvantaged in their ability to raise funds from foundations? Several explanations seem plausible. Feminist groups are the most recent entrants into the political process, and they appeared in a period of economic downturn.[17] In addition, most foundations are dominated by men at both board and staff levels, and they have not given priority to women's issues.[18] Groups such as NOW and others may be perceived as having a "radical" image or may be caught in a "Catch 22" situation without an established "track record" and, lacking funds, inability to get one.[19]

Despite limited foundation support, feminist groups have grown substantially since the 1976 study cited above. While still grossly underfinanced, feminists have gained some access to foundation as well as government funding, and several feminist groups more than doubled their incomes in the late 1970s. Although financial problems remain crucial, many groups have experienced growth over the past decade, as measured both by expanding staff and by increasing funding. CWPS tripled its grants, from \$200,000 in 1978 to \$600,000 in 1979.[20] Groups like the WEAL Fund and NOW-LDEF have grown from office operations with one professional staff person and volunteer aides several years ago to operations with several paid professionals and support staff.

Foundation support comprises at least half the annual budget

[16] *Survey of Six Foundations that Derive their Assets Primarily from Sales of Cosmetics to Women* (New York: Women and Foundations/Corporate Philanthropy, April 1978).

[17] See *Financial Support of Women's Programs in the 1970's*, 23, and Tully, "Funding the Feminists," 28-30.

[18] *Balancing the Scales of Justice*, 95.

[19] Karen O'Connor, *Women's Organizations: Use of the Courts* (Lexington, Mass.: D. C. Heath, 1980), 119.

[20] Interview with Jane Chapman, CWPS, Oct. 10, 1979.

for several groups and a significant portion for the others. This dependency creates problems for feminist groups, while at the same time this funding has permitted the groups' very existence and expansion in the past decade. As suggested above, foundations tend to favor funding established groups, significantly limiting possibilities for aiding feminist groups. Second, foundations tend to donate money on a project basis or for issue areas for a specified period of time. Few groups analyzed here are able to gain substantial general unrestricted funding. This pattern of funding tends to limit both the scope and the flexibility of groups, which are then locked into those projects deemed fundable. Several groups examined have become involved in projects they would not have undertaken had special funds not been made available for specific studies or conferences. Many group leaders feel that foundations prefer to fund educational programs and are loath to fund litigation. Leaders of other groups indicated that foundations were fond of funding such things as internship programs, which were sometimes of limited value in contributing to fulfillment of organizational goals. Some groups have accepted money for "earmarked" projects and have sought to utilize them "loosely" in order to gain flexibility. In general, funding may shape a group's entire focus and distort its initial priorities.[21] Project-by-project funding fragments an organization and hinders a holistic approach to policy development. Finally, it is unclear what methods are used by foundations to determine the success of their ventures. The "follow-up" and evaluation techniques used in many instances seem haphazard at best and call into question the rationality of allocation processes.

Because foundations are such a major source of support, a decrease in their funding of an organization may have adverse consequences. In 1979 the Ford Foundation cut its appropri-

---

[21] *Balancing the Scales of Justice*, 107.

ations to some groups and warned of further cutbacks.[22] All groups must compete with one another and with newer groups for the same (increasingly) scarce resources. Put in somewhat different terms, funding continues to be a serious problem for all groups, particularly in an era of inflation.

Although most groups have been creative in their efforts to augment traditional sources of funding, this is not an easy task. One feminist group that relies heavily on one government agency and one foundation (Ford) for its funding was rebuffed in 1979 by virtually every other new source approached.[23]

Membership

Membership too may be a valuable resource. For the feminist community, the issue of constituency remains a controversial one. In 1978 NARAL, NWPC, WEAL, and NOW had a combined dues-paying membership of about 250,000—a substantial increase from 75,000-80,000 in 1971.[24] NOW and NARAL, in particular, increased their paid membership dramatically. Nonetheless, members of these groups still comprise but a small segment of women in the United States. Several leaders and policy makers interviewed for this study emphasized the importance of constituency-based groups, arguing that the absence of such mass organizations significantly weakens efforts to influence policy at every level of the political process. Even (and perhaps especially) at the administrative level, the image of organizational strength may aid in changing an agency's perspective and priorities through the development of a new constituency. For example, analysis of Title VI of the

[22] *Foundation Grants Index, Bi-Monthly* (March/April 1979), G87. In December 1980 the Ford Foundation announced that it was doubling its grants for women's activities, from $4 million to $9 million a year. It is not clear what percentage of these funds will be directed to the groups considered in this study. *Women in the World* (New York: Ford Foundation, Nov. 1980).

[23] WEAL Fund, *1979 Development Highlights*, Nov. 1979.

[24] Maren Lockwood Carden, *The New Feminist Movement* (New York: Russell Sage, 1974), 140.

Civil Rights Act of 1964 enforcement suggests that civil rights groups greatly increased their political effectiveness when they belatedly began to mobilize and represent their mass constituency.[25]

The concern for a mass base has been expressed by scholars and activists alike. One student of feminist politics worried about the gap she discerned between active feminists and constituents, observing that isolation from the grassroots often produces policy commitments out of touch with actual mass needs.[26] The leadership of at least one group examined (WLDF) determined that it had to develop a membership base because such a course would increase accountability, credibility, and funding capacity. It is undeniable that as laws and their regulations reach the stage of implementation in issue areas such as education, grassroots efforts provide the information on compliance or noncompliance as well as the general feedback necessary to determine to what extent the laws are effective. In another context, "pro-choice" forces, routed continually in legislative efforts in recent years (although not always in the courts), have turned increasingly to constituency-building, partially to replicate the success of "right-to-life" groups that so effectively have organized at the community level and have brought pressure to bear in state and national legislative politics and at the ballot box.

But building membership also requires servicing it in some fashion; frequently groups barely break even as a result of mailing newsletters and other materials. In addition, membership expressing its wishes via annual conventions or other mechanisms may limit organizational flexibility and maneuverability in the political process. It is difficult to engage in compromise—as most groups in the feminist group matrix

[25] See Gary Orfield, *Reconstruction of Southern Education* (New York: Wiley, 1969), 122; Beryl Radin, *Implementation, Change and the Federal Bureaucracy* (New York: Columbia University Teachers College Press, 1977).

[26] Margaret Berger, "Litigation on Behalf of Women: An Assessment," unpublished manuscript prepared for the Ford Foundation (March 12, 1979), 87, and personal discussions, Dec. 1979 and Jan. 1980.

customarily do—when an emotional issue is at stake and when leadership must be accountable to members. Mass issues often tend to create opposing constituencies, and as more emotions are inflamed and media attention focused on an issue, change-oriented groups such as feminists may well lose out. Moreover, feminist groups face major obstacles to organizational recruitment; they face the "free rider" problem. Under such circumstances, organization-building is especially difficult.

It seems that the benefits of membership organizations are significant but that highly specialized lobbying, research, and litigation groups also perform key functions in our highly fragmented political system. At this juncture, feminists may have the best of both worlds in that they may call upon membership without necessarily incurring the cost of maintaining it through their relationships with traditional women's groups and a public generally supportive of equal rights. Whether feminists can continue to rely on this de facto constituency may be a major question for the 1980s.

Techniques for Exerting Political Influence

Techniques used by feminist groups are reformist and involve traditional approaches to advocacy, lobbying, litigation, and monitoring. The flexibility with which groups approach political activity is notable; they will use any technique that has promise, and they will change tactics if necessary. There are, of course, several favored techniques for influencing the political process.

Protest

In contrast to the civil rights movement in the late fifties and early sixties, protest has never been a dominant method for feminists. NOW activists disrupted a 1970 Senate Judiciary Subcommittee meeting in order to dramatize the demand for the ERA, and at the state level some demonstrations in support of state ERA ratification have been held. In 1970 a mass rally, "Women's Strike for Equality," was held around the nation, bringing together disparate elements in the movement to advocate day care, abortion on demand, and equal education and employment opportunity.

More recent demonstrations of militancy have been limited. Equity-oriented feminists saw them as unnecessary in part because other channels of access to the political system were opened without much difficulty in the 1970s. Perhaps one reason for this *relative* openness in the political system is that women comprise a majority of the population in the nation and many politicians perceive that potentially they comprise a formidable bloc that *may* vote on women's issues. Also, sympathetic and articulate women in Congress (Martha Griffiths, Bella Abzug, Margaret Heckler, and Elizabeth Holtzman), legislative aides to members of Congress, and administrative staff members in the bureaucracy provided access to women's groups before, during, and after the passage by Congress of the ERA.

Litigation

While litigation has been employed by feminist groups, it too has never occupied the central role it did for civil rights groups. There is no feminist group comparable to the NAACP Legal Defense and Educational Fund in funding and status, although the combined legal resources of the two ACLU women's related programs make the ACLU a major force for litigation. The use of *pro bono* attorneys has been less well developed by feminists, despite the fact that general resources or resources earmarked for litigation have been hard to come by. Funds for "special projects" have been more readily available from foundations and other contributors. One reason for feminist restraint regarding the use of litigation may be that the Supreme Court has never declared sex to be a suspect classification in the same manner as race, thus making judicial victory uncertain.

Groups that specialize in law-related activities spend a good deal of time on actual litigation, although increasingly even their work has come to include other activities, such as educating the public, gathering and disseminating information, analyzing and drafting legislation, commenting and testifying on proposed regulations, and monitoring enforcement. For example, the director of one litigation group interviewed for this study estimated that she devotes only 20 percent of her time to actual litigation; another feminist attorney gave 40 percent as her estimate.

Litigation is seen as a mechanism for developing case law and precedents for an entire class and as a "consciousness raiser" for the public and the political system even if a case is lost. Cases also are seen as having a "spillover effect" on the private and public sector beyond the confines of a particular suit. Thus *General Electric* v. *Gilbert*,[27] which dealt with pregnancy disability, was lost by feminists in the Supreme Court in 1976 but provided a catalyst for coalition-building in the Congress, leading ultimately to the enactment of the Pregnancy Disability Act, which amended Title VII of the Civil Rights Act of 1964. The ACLU Reproductive Freedom Project (together with other groups) pressed for a judicial ruling against the Hyde amendment in *Harris* v. *McRae*[28]; perhaps the 1980 feminist defeat in this case will galvanize new political efforts. After success in *Reed* v. *Reed*[29] and *Frontiero* v. *Richardson*,[30] in 1975 the ACLU Women's Rights Project successfully fought gender-based discrimination in the awarding of social security benefits in *Weinberger* v. *Weisenfeld*[31] and gained increased court recognition of the need for a "higher standard of review" in subsequent cases on sex-discrimination issues relating to social security and welfare.

In addition to setting precedents, litigation is also used as a tool to prod the political process into action regarding enforcement, by establishing seriousness of purpose and credi-

[27] 429 U.S. 129 (1976).
[28] 491 F. Supp. 630 (1980).
[29] 404 U.S. 71 (1971).
[30] 411 U.S. 677 (1973).
[31] 420 U.S. 636 (1975).

bility. Thus in *WEAL* v. *Califano*[32] attorneys from the CLASP Women's Rights Project sought compliance with Title IX of the Education Amendments of 1972 regarding sex equity in education (settled in 1977). Some observers attribute the final release of Title IX athletic guidelines in 1979, which were favorable to feminists, to their efforts to obtain a contempt citation against HEW for continued nonenforcement. Although the contempt citation was dismissed by the presiding judge, its existence may have served as a form of pressure to hasten the release of the long-overdue new guidelines. (Feminists were opposed on this issue by the National Collegiate Athletic Association and a coalition of college and university presidents.)[33]

Some litigation groups do little actual litigation because of their limited funds. They must often rely on outside counsel— preferably *pro bono*—to do their actual case work. These groups tend to become involved in suits primarily through the filing of *amicus* briefs. NOW-LDEF, WLDF, and WEAL are among those whose litigation efforts have been limited by inadequate resources.

As litigation costs have risen and funding for litigation has become more limited and more dispersed among nonprofit groups (for example, CLASP and others have been severely cut back by the Ford Foundation), and as effort expended on cases and appeals appears to become more and more protracted and burdensome, it is not surprising that groups have sought other techniques to achieve their goals.

Lobbying and Monitoring

Virtually all of the groups analyzed here now do some legislative (and administrative) lobbying since the relaxation of Internal Revenue Service rules that now permit even 501(c)(3) groups to lobby up to 20 percent of their time. Hence legislative drafting, expert testimony, negotiations with members

---

[32] U.S. Dist. Ct. for D. of C., Civ. Act no. 70-3095 (1977).
[33] Interview with Cindy Brown, former Deputy Director, Office of Civil Rights, HEW, Nov. 13, 1979.

of Congress, and dissemination of research have become part of the daily activity for nearly all feminist groups. Feminist groups have been active in the legislative arena ever since their successful efforts to secure passage of the Equal Credit Opportunity Act and the Pregnancy Disability Act and their success in having prevented weakening amendments and riders from emasculating Title IX of the Education Amendments of 1972. With regard to the Hyde amendments and other "pro-life" legislation that have in successive years systematically limited federal payments for abortions, they have been less successful, but nonetheless persistent.

Advocacy and monitoring at the agency level have increased for all groups with the recognition of the importance of the administrative process in sustaining and consolidating legislative and judicial gains. Supplying information, commenting on proposed regulations, and the monitoring of enforcement policy is now common for all groups. Because federal agencies—some newly created, others now pursuing missions different from their original assignments—have been operating in a variety of new issue areas, groups with constituency or informational resources have often been able to play a key role. In fact, several groups devote themselves primarily to research, recognizing the impact that informational resources may have on policy development. Thus CWPS was founded to provide a scholarly research focus for the feminist movement and has published several books documenting economic and other kinds of discrimination against women. Most groups publish newsletters or informational flyers. Among them are *In the Running*, a quarterly publication of WEAL Fund's SPRINT, and the ACLU-WRP's *Women's Rights Report*. Many groups issue frequent reviews of federal policy affecting their particular area of interest, disseminated to members (if any) and interested citizens. Special publications issued by groups serve to prod the policy process into action by calling attention to failures of enforcement and commitment of resources. Particularly notable was PEER's *Stalled at the Start*, a critique of HEW's enforcement of Title IX. This document received considerable publicity and dissemination when it was issued in 1978. An ACLU-RFP Report on the *Impact of the Hyde Amendment on Federally Funded Abortions* (1978) documented the virtual elimination of such abortions (almost 100 percent) since passage of the initial congressional amendment.

Many of the groups discussed here are recognized as being expert in their field, and they are asked by policy makers to prepare analyses of existing or proposed legislation or regulations or to assess the impact of existing rules and laws. Many serve as informational clearinghouses to which elected and appointed officials, other interest groups, and the general public turn for specific information and data. SPRINT responds to numerous requests by phone or mail regarding sex equity in education and sports. WLDF responded to 3,469 requests for information in 1977, up from 2,000 in the previous year. Other groups providing such services include the CWPS, NARAL (which answers over one hundred letters per week), and ACLU-WRP.[34]

Constituency Organizing and Leadership Training

Several groups including CLASP, WEAL Fund, NARAL, and NOW-LDEF have internship programs that have the dual function of training new practitioners for the feminist movement and obtaining additional workers at reduced cost. The ACLU-WRP originated with a clinic at Columbia University Law School, which it still maintains. CLASP has twenty-five student interns each semester and relations with nine law schools. Individuals who have received training within feminist groups often remain as staff members in these groups or are employed in related government or advocacy organizations where their skills and expertise prove invaluable. Virtually all groups hold seminars and conduct lectures for lawyers, students, and others on a wide range of feminist issues.

---

[34] WLDF, *Annual Report, June 1978-July 1979*, Appendix 2; WCLU-WRP, quarterly reports; interview with Karen Mulhauser, NARAL, Oct. 10, 1979. The WRP reports almost 1,000 annual requests.

These functions sensitize large groups of people to feminist approaches and issue concerns.

Organizations like NOW that have mass memberships are, of course, involved with constituency organizing and relations. In addition, several other organizations maintain community-organizing components. The Women's Rights Project of the ACLU has an office in Richmond, Virginia, which is concerned with organizing, public education, and bringing grassroots cases to the attention of the New York office. This ACLU effort exists because of a specific bequest establishing a Southern office. NARAL has sought to build a grassroots constituency through direct mail because of a belief that the best way to combat the "right-to-life" opposition is to emulate its strategy of developing constituency strength. WLDF is eager to build a membership organization, partially to develop financial independence but also "to provide accountability— to assure that the Fund takes positions which have support in a national feminist community"—and to "provide a base" for referring women throughout the country to feminist-oriented attorneys and counsellors.[35] Many groups use grassroots activity to aid the enforcement process. PEER has sought to develop monitoring strength at the grassroots for Title IX through the dissemination of a local action kit called *Cracking the Glass Slipper*, emulating a technique pioneered by NOW in its issuance of equal credit kits, which provides instruction on how to assess discrimination and file complaints. Finally, all groups discussed devote considerable time and effort to internal administration and fund-raising.

Leadership and Coalition-Building

As suggested earlier, feminists have been able to rely on a preexisting structure of traditional women's groups (such as the League of Women Voters and General Federation of Women's Clubs) whose shared interest in many feminist issues has

[35] Women's Legal Defense Board, "Report on Long-Range Planning of the WLDF Board of Directors (Washington, D.C., n.d.)," unpublished report, 8-9.

produced numbers and assistance that would otherwise have been costly and probably unattainable. The civil rights movement served as a model of structure and tactics and provided considerable assistance to the incipient feminist movement as it developed. Indeed, some legislative gains by feminist groups have involved use of civil rights legislation; for example, Title VII of the Civil Rights Act of 1964 (provisions against race and sex discrimination) was amended to include pregnancy disability insurance protection. Feminist successes, in turn, have helped other groups: the Equal Credit Opportunity Act served as a model for minorities and the aged, who lobbied to amend the law to cover their groups as well.

Despite the existence of numerous autonomous subgroupings that compete for funding and influence, there is, as noted previously, extensive coalition-building and remarkable unity among feminists. Individuals and groups join together in a variety of contexts linked by loose commitment to feminist ideology, shared symbols of group identity, and the friendships and contacts they have developed.

There is no one central point of contact, but there are intersecting sets of personal relationships and other intergroup exchanges that provide a network for common activity. Friendships among group activists as well as multiple group memberships provide linkages and facilitate the sharing of information, the mobilization of activity on specific projects, and the planning of joint strategy. Groups also come together at meetings, rallies, and conferences.[36] The movement for the ERA and more recent state and national meetings for the International Women's Year (1977) served this function, too. Communications media within the movement provide links regarding issues, projects, and activities, while issue specialists form their own subunits for sharing information.

Feminist coalitions with varying degrees of institutionalization and permanency exist for a number of issue areas: for

[36] Joan Cassell, *A Group Called Women* (New York: McKay, 1977), ch. 8.

example, regarding educational equality, there is the National Coalition for Women and Girls in Education; for abortion rights, there is the "pro-choice" caucus; and there are coalitions on women and health, women and poverty, and women in the military. Ad hoc coalitions are created as necessary both within the movement and with allied groups. An example of this phenomenon was the Coalition to End Discrimination Against Pregnant Workers, in which representatives of 300 groups comprised largely of feminists and labor unionists successfully persuaded Congress to amend Title VII of the Civil Rights Act of 1964 to include pregnancy as an insured healthcare benefit. A newer group, the Coalition for Reproductive Rights of Women, seeks to prevent employers from using classifications of "hazardous employment" to bar only women from holding specific jobs. The Coalition to End Discrimination Against Pregnant Workers may be characterized, in Berry's terms, as "participatory," with no one dominant group, resource commitment from many groups, and temporary existence. Others, such as the National Coalition for Women and Girls in Education, are "independent"; the Education coalition has permanence and a letterhead, although several groups (AIAW, CLASP-WRP, WEAL Fund, and ACE) have tended to play major roles within it.[37] In addition, feminists have also joined together in the Washington Women's Network, Coalition on Women Appointments, and the Judicial Selection Panel. Thus they have consciously engaged in network-building and have created an effective mechanism for both specialization and cohesion.

Effectiveness of the movement is enhanced by division of labor; differing goals and approaches have not caused permanent splits or paralysis. There are particular people whose personalities are well suited to coordination and providing informational feedback and resources. Thus people such as Judith Lichtman, WLDF's executive director, help bring groups together as well. Networking—consciously facilitated by fem-

[37] See Berry, *Lobbying for the People*, 257-60.

inists—has both positive and negative features. While it may retard efforts at seeking immediate tangible goals when concerted action is necessary, ultimate success may be more likely because flexibility and experimentation are encouraged. In fact, the movement is capable of energetic action through intergroup mobilization when necessary, as the Pregnancy Disability Act case demonstrates.

Finally, another example of coalition behavior among feminist groups is to be found in what may be termed "interlocking directorates." A striking feature of many of the groups considered is the overlapping memberships of their boards (people who hold formal staff or board positions in one or more groups). These persons serve as links between organizations because of their dual (and sometimes multiple) memberships in feminist groups. Table 6 illustrates these overlapping memberships. In addition, organizations are also found as each other's clients; for example, CLASP attorneys represented WEAL in its suit *WEAL* v. *Califano*.

CONCLUSION

In this chapter we have suggested that despite the existence of significant deficiencies in their resources, among them limited funding and membership from potential constituents, feminists have been creative in the utilization of those resources they do possess. Among the latter are dedicated and committed staff personnel and creative and pragmatic use of existing funds. Feminists have exercised flexibility in choosing strategies and approaches and have employed traditional pressure-group tactics with considerable skill, as the four case studies that follow demonstrate to varying degrees. Finally, the simultaneous reliance on groups' specialization and coalition activity has maximized the effective use of existing resources.

TABLE 6
Interlocking Directorates among Feminist Groups (1978)

	WLDF	NOW-LDEF	NWPC	ACLU	CWPS	WEAL	CLASP	NARAL
Barbara Bergmann	•					•	•	
Jessie Bernard	•					•		
Margaret Gates					•	•		
Ruth B. Ginsburg		*	•	•	•	•		•
Krysten Horbal							•	
Margaret Kohn			•					•
Odessa Komer	•						•	
Brooksley Landau		•						
Sylvia Law	•			•		•		
Judith Lichtman				•				
Margaret Moses				•		•		•
Harriet Pilpel				•		•		
Bernice "Bunny" Sandler†								
Diana Steele				•		•		
Gloria Steinem			•			•		•

Source: Annual reports and personal interviews.
* Once director.
† Director, Project on the Status and Education of Women of the American Association of Colleges.

CHAPTER 4

WOMEN AND CREDIT DISCRIMINATION

INTRODUCTION

In 1974 Congress passed, and the President signed into law, the Equal Credit Opportunity Act (ECOA), which banned credit discrimination on the basis of sex. One year later, in October 1975, regulations promulgated by the Federal Reserve Board were completed, and the provisions of the 1974 law were implemented. The history of the Act's passage and implementation provides us with a good example of specialization on issues and formation of coalitions among women's groups as they worked to achieve very specific equity goals in both the congressional and administrative arenas.

It can be argued that activist women were able to place the issue of credit reform to eliminate sex discrimination on the political agenda because they adhered effectively to the prerequisites of the "mobilization of bias" or existing configuration of influence and access to power. Seen in this light, women succeeded in winning significant credit reforms not because they violated the "rules of the game," but because they conformed to them so well. From this perspective, the ability of women activists to achieve their goals is not necessarily proof of the openness of the system, but rather an indication of its elitist nature. In a political universe in which the critics of pluralist theory have argued that participants speak with a decidedly upper-middle-class accent, the women seeking credit reform were of high social status[1]; and in a

---

[1] Maren Lockwood Carden, *The New Feminist Movement* (New York: Russell Sage, 1974), 19-20.

political system in which access and representation of one's interests at key points in the decision-making process are crucial, an ongoing "policy system" served the cause of women's rights well.[2] Women activists understood the need for effective use of the media, organizational skill, and expert testimony. In additition, they possessed respectability and a high degree of technical competence, as well as a spirit of group efficiency and unity.[3] Women activists also understood the need to keep the issue under control by limiting its scope—in order to maximize rather than dissipate their resources. Although equal credit opportunity is an issue with profound long-term implications, it was perceived as a role equity issue, and as such it threatened no fundamental values.

There would probably not be an Equal Credit Opportunity Act were it not for the actions of some women's groups. Thus the legislative and later the administrative efforts of these women clearly indicate success. There was not, however, a total victory inasmuch as women's groups had to accept a compromise both in Congress and later at the Federal Reserve Board. Janette Hart, of the Federal Reserve Board's Office of Saver and Consumer Affairs, the body responsible for the administrative regulations for the ECOA, made the above distinction. Throughout the process leading to the enactment of the credit law, representatives of women's groups recognized the nature of incremental politics in the United States and understood the need to compromise. Thus they did not place themselves in support of extreme positions from which they could not deviate with relative ease.

It should be noted that the women's community was united on the ECOA; traditional women's groups were highly supportive of activist groups in their pressure for the enactment and writing of favorable regulations for the Act. While not involved as active lobbyists, they were (as it will be discussed

[2] David Truman, *The Governmental Process* (New York: Knopf, 1951), 322-32.

[3] Darryl Baskin, *American Pluralist Democracy: A Critique* (New York: Van Nostrand-Reinhold, 1971), 92.

later in this analysis) supporters of credit legislation favorable to women and helped create a coalition that gave the appearance of considerable support for the ECOA.

BACKGROUND

Students of the legislative process have argued in recent years that new policies are adopted after a change in opinion, not as a result of group pressures.[4] In fact, several studies have raised doubts about the effectiveness of pressure groups in the legislative process. Viewed from this perspective, women's groups might be expected to play only a negligible role in legislative politics. This section will attempt to demonstrate, however, that despite significant limitations on staff and financial resources, women activists were able to initiate and sustain momentum for legislative action on equal credit opportunity. As one member of Congress put it: "Without the input of women activists pushing for credit reform, there would be no Equal Credit Opportunity Act."

Perhaps because interest in this issue had been heightened by a National Commission on Consumer Finance and subsequent media coverage, making many members of congress more responsive to the issue, women activists were able to keep it alive for two congressional terms. Women's organizations supplied information, technical expertise, and explicit suggestions on policy to members of Congress. Unlike the campaign to adopt the Equal Rights Amendment, which had a broad scope and vast constituency as well as organized opposition, the efforts made for the passage of legislation on equal credit opportunity were primarily at a leadership level with only a limited amount of grassroots involvement.[5] But, as Jo Freeman suggests, the movement for equal credit opportunity was able to build upon the contacts created during

[4] James Q. Wilson, *Political Organizations* (New York: Basic Books, 1973), 330.

[5] Jo Freeman, *The Politics of Women's Liberation* (New York: David McKay, 1975), 217.

the long fight for the ERA. That battle had, in her words, created a new "policy system," involving lobbyists, volunteers, members of Congress and their staffs, and policy makers in the administrative sector.[6]

The success of advocates of credit reform may also be attributed in part to the existence of a "policy vacuum" in an area of few established political precedents as well as to a lack of clear political opposition. Representatives of industry were aware of the extent of credit afforded women by way of male co-signers and were cognizant of the potential credit worthiness of women. Thus there was apparently some concern by the representatives of industry not to antagonize groups of women on what was perceived as an *equity* issue.

In addition, members of Congress were sensitive to reactions of the potentially active women's groups in their local constituencies.[7] The majority of women vote; many women work in political campaigns. Some local NWPC groups made credit a (local) campaign issue. It is important to recognize that women activists acted as a vanguard, causing legislators to operate in anticipation of voters' reactions and thus to act somewhat in advance of mass consciousness on the issue. However, by 1974, it was apparent that the majority of women had become aware of the credit discrimination they suffered. The 1974 *Virginia Slims American Women's Opinion Poll* indicated that 57 percent of American women believed that women suffered credit discrimination.[8]

THE PROBLEM OF CREDIT DISCRIMINATION

"Hormones, birth control and wedding rings are not matters of credit." When Betty Furness spoke these words before the Subcommittee on Consumer Affairs of the Committee on

[6] *Ibid.*, 220.

[7] Gary Orfield, *Congressional Power: Congress and Social Change* (New York: Harcourt-Brace-Jovanovich, 1975), 305.

[8] *Virginia Slims American Women's Opinion Poll*, Vol. III (New York: Roper Organization, 1975), 5.

Banking and Currency of the House of Representatives in November 1973, she expressed the concerns of the thousands of American women who had been denied credit in their own names as a result of being female.

Discrimination against women because of their sex and marital status had been institutionalized over the years by the credit industry. This discrimination was rooted in a "long standing tradition, outmoded customs, beliefs and attitudes fraught with myth."[9] Whereas in the eighteenth and nineteenth centuries it was not customary for married women with sufficient means to qualify for credit to work, this was no longer the rule in modern society. In 1973 over 40 percent of the nation's labor force was female, and many women worked to provide the sole or major source of income for themselves and their families. Assumptions upon which the credit industry rested its unequal treatment of women were simply no longer true: that all women stop working when they have children; that working mothers are delinquent on payment of bills; that divorced women rely exclusively on unstable support from former husbands; and the like.

In March 1973 42 percent of married women worked (up from 26 percent in 1953).[10] A third of mothers with children under 6 were in the labor force, as were half of the women whose children were between 6 and 17 years of age.[11] In the 22 million families in which husbands and wives both worked, family income had been substantially raised. Women were the heads of 6 million families and, in 1971, 54 percent of them were in the labor force.[12] As of March 1971, 70 percent of all divorced and 50 percent of all separated women were in

[9] Statement of the National Organization for Women before the Subcommittee on Consumer Affairs of the Committee on Banking and Currency, House of Representatives, mimeo., Nov. 13, 1973, 1.

[10] Howard Hayghe, "Marital and Family Characteristics of the Labor Force in March 1973," *Monthly Labor Review* 97 (April 1974), 21.

[11] *Ibid.*, 23.

[12] Elizabeth Waldman and Kathryn R. Gover, "Marital and Family Characteristics of the Labor Force," *Monthly Labor Review* 95 (April 1972), 6.

the labor force (and these women, if working at age 35, had a work expectancy of 27-29 years!).[13] A 1969 study by the Women's Bureau of the Department of Labor found that labor turnover is influenced more by job level, age, record of stability, and length of service than by sex; also, differences in job turnover between men and women are small.[14] In addition, although there is scant research on the subject, available studies indicate that women are good credit risks.[15]

However, despite the changing social and economic role of women, they continued to be treated as "second-class citizens" by the credit industry. Surveys of the lending policies of banks and of savings and loan associations found that few of them would grant full credit to a working wife's income.[16] Single women also had difficulty qualifying for credit. In one classic example, a 40-year-old woman was required to have her father co-sign a bank loan.[17] Married women lacked a credit history since all records were kept in their husbands' names. In order to obtain credit, they often were forced to respond to humiliating questions regarding birth-control techniques and intent to bear children. Divorced and widowed women were subject

[13] *Ibid.*, 7.

[14] U. S. Department of Labor (Women's Bureau), *Facts about Women's Absenteeism and Labor Turnover* (Washington, D.C.: Government Printing Office, 1969), 2-3, 15.

[15] For both married and single women, bad account probability is less than for men with similar marital status. Paul Smith, "Measuring Risk on Installment Credit," *Management Science* 2 (Nov. 1964), 324-40. And, as the percentage of the family income earned by the husband decreases, delinquency in mortgage payments decreases. Leon Kendall, *Anatomy of the Residential Mortgage Market* (Washington, D.C.: U.S. Savings and Loan League, 1964), 59. According to J. Harzog and J. Earley, working wives are no more prone to delinquency and foreclosure than other borrowers. *Home Mortgage Delinquency and Foreclosure* (New York: National Bureau of Economic Research, 1970). In a communication to Jane Roberts Chapman and Margaret Gates of CWPS, Thomas Jones, executive director of Neighborhood Housing Services, Inc., found the mortgage delinquency rate among female-headed families to be 2 percent as opposed to 4 percent for the total group.

[16] *New York Times*, March 25, 1973, 1.

[17] Margaret Smith, "Where Credit is Due," *Ms*, Oct. 1972, 36.

to particular discrimination. Alimony and child support as well as other monetary resources were ignored as income when these women applied for credit. The need to alter the discriminatory treatment of women in the credit-granting process first received national attention in May 1972 at the hearings of the National Commission on Consumer Finance.

When the National Commission on Consumer Finance held these hearings to determine the extent of the problems relating to the entire area of consumer credit, among the issues they sought to examine was credit discrimination based upon sex and marital status. Extensive testimony pointed up the conditions relegating women to an inferior legal status as far as the availability and receipt of credit were concerned. The hearings underlined five specific areas of difficulty for women seeking credit. It was determined that single women had more trouble obtaining credit than single men; creditors generally required a woman upon marriage to reapply for credit, usually in her husband's name (whereas similar reapplication was not demanded of men when they married); creditors were often unwilling to extend credit to a married woman in her own name, or to count the wife's income when a married couple applied for credit; and women who were divorced or widowed had trouble reestablishing personal credit.[18]

The Commission's hearings created a rippling effect that has never stopped. Once the situation was accepted as a problem, and the extent of legal inferiority was clearly articulated, the movement for the passage of corrective legislation began.

The reality of credit discrimination attracted great attention from several national women's groups and a number of congressional leaders. Media coverage was extensive—both in the press and in women's magazines—throughout the nation and accentuated the growing interest in the problem. Women's groups, public interest organizations, and human rights commissions undertook credit surveys, which rein-

[18] National Commission on Consumer Finance, *Consumer Credit in the United States* (Washington, D.C.: Government Printing Office, 1972), 498-99.

forced the fact of pervasive credit discrimination everywhere. "Credit kits" were prepared by NOW chapters and local women's organizations to educate women on the problem and to stimulate action. Many women became aware of the fact that the discrimination they had faced was not simply a personal experience but, rather, represented part of a pattern of discrimination against over half of the American population. As a shared problem, it became an issue around which women's interests and energies could be mobilized.

The woman most instrumental during the initial period in facilitating cooperation among women's groups and fostering interest in the issue in Congress was Sharyn Campbell, an attorney who, at this time, was the chairwoman of the NOW Task Force on Consumer Credit. During the legislative and administrative process, various other members of NOW emerged as leaders in the quest for equal credit opportunity. (It should be noted that although NOW does have a legislative lobbying office in Washington, this office never participated in the struggle for equal credit. That it did not was due to intragroup factionalism within the organization, pitting a faction loyal to then President Karen DeCrow against the press and legislative offices. Hence the extensive resources of NOW were not available to those members who took a strong stand on equal credit opportunity.) In addition to NOW members, a second group, the Center for Women Policy Studies, played a major role in providing the technical expertise utilized by women's groups. A nonprofit research group, the Center had received a $40,000 grant from the Ford Foundation in order to develop information on the relative role of women as credit risks. When the demands of the legislative and administrative process made it clear that the original issue was no longer as relevant as it had been, Ford permitted the (primarily) two-woman operation to turn its attention to aiding in the formulation of a credit law. The input of the Center was invaluable to the women's cause because the quality of their work came to be highly respected by both legislators and later by the staff attorneys at the Federal Reserve Board (the administrative agency charged with writing the credit regulations); the Center's lawyers were viewed as responsible and reasonable professionals at all levels of the political process. The Center provided most of the background expertise, while women lobbyists determined the strategy to be followed throughout.

Not only was support for the elimination of credit discrimination forthcoming from women's rights groups, but also the credit industry itself was not belligerent, and many members of Congress were supportive. There was, in fact, no strong opposition to the concept of passage of *some* legislation that would eliminate sex discrimination in credit, although the exact form of such a law was controversial.

In part, the tacit agreement among members of the industry and Congress that some protective legislation was in the offing was a testament to the perceived strength of the women's rights movement. This movement had been legitimized politically by the battle for the ERA, which convinced many members of Congress that support for women's rights could engender significant electoral support in campaigns.[19] Because discrimination in credit-granting was an issue of potential importance to all women, members of Congress were aware of its widespread appeal. In addition, because the issue was not one involving any outlay of public funds, it was easy for legislators to support, particularly in a preelection period. As for the credit industry, it had been made aware of the problems in extension of credit to women and feared a poor public image. This is not intended to suggest that industry welcomed credit regulations with open arms. At the outset of the movement for the passage of legislation, many industry spokesmen were a bit defensive. However, most members of the credit industry recognized that some legislation would be enacted. It was clear that support for legislation was, if not totally positive on the Hill, at least not negative. Hence the industry would not publicly argue the merits of enacting legislation,

[19] Freeman, *Politics of Women's Liberation*, 171; see also Theodore J. Lowi, *The End of Liberalism* (New York: Norton, 1969), 69.

although it would work behind the scenes for desired provisions and testify at legislative hearings to clarify its position. In the long run, the industry must have felt that the extension of credit to more credit-worthy female recipients would be beneficial to business.

LEGISLATIVE INTERACTIONS

At the same time that the National Commission on Consumer Finance was holding its hearings, Representative Bella Abzug (D–N.Y.) introduced legislation—co-sponsored by over one hundred members of the House of Representatives—dealing with several aspects of credit discrimination. Her bills served as the initial thrust within Congress for the gathering momentum of women's groups pressuring for legislation to end credit discrimination, despite the fact that this legislative proposal never was adopted.

Early Congressional Considerations

In January 1973 several bills amending the Truth in Lending Act, to prohibit discrimination on the basis of sex and marital status, were introduced in the Senate. The bills, one of which was introduced by Senator William Brock (R–Tenn.), differed with respect to maximum levels of recovery in class actions. Senator Brock's bill had a lower level of maximum liability in class-action suits than other bills that were introduced. He hoped to gain support from liberals who could accept the lower class-action levels and thus back his bill, which broadly defined credit and abandoned attempts to define discrimination.[20] Many of the activist women who were involved in these legislative efforts from the outset accepted his limitations on recovery in class actions.

Senator Brock was a relatively conservative Republican from Tennessee with a rating in 1974 (on a scale where 100 means perfect liberal ideological conformity) of 20 from the Amer-

---

[20] Nancy Polikoff, "Legislative Solutions to Sex Discrimination in Credit," *Women's Rights Law Reporter* 2 (July 1974), 31.

icans for Democratic Action and of 86 from the Americans for Conservative Action.[21] His role in introducing equal credit legislation, and subsequently acting as floor leader for the bill, can be explained by reference to his own political experiences. As a member of the National Commission on Consumer Finance, he became sensitive to the need to legislate an end to the discriminatory practices suffered by women. Furthermore, on his staff was a feminist political scientist, Emily Card, who apparently was able to transfer her support and enthusiasm for equal credit legislation to Senator Brock. She drafted the initial legislation and acted as a gadfly in promoting the cause of credit reform. When the Senator's preliminary efforts met with resistance from industry, according to Ms. Card, he became even more convinced of the need for such credit reform legislation.

Senator Brock proved to be an excellent sponsor for the equal credit opportunity legislation in 1973 (included in the Truth in Lending Act amendments of that year). In part because he was a conservative member of the Senate, he was able to gain the crucial support of many of his fellow Republicans who might not ordinarily have agreed to such a measure. When the legislation came to the Senate floor in July 1973 (without hearings), it passed 90 to 0. This bill simply stated:

> It shall be unlawful for any credit or card issuer to discriminate on account of sex or marital status against any individual with respect to the approval or denial of any extension of consumer credit or with respect to the approval, denial, renewal, continuation, or revocation of any open end consumer credit account or with respect to the terms thereof.[22]

It also awarded punitive damages of $10,000 or 10 percent of net worth, whichever is less, in class-action suits.

Representative Margaret Heckler (R–Mass.) introduced the

---

[21] *Congressional.Quarterly Weekly Report* 32 (March 30, 1974), 815.

[22] *Congressional Record*, July 23, 1973, S. 14431.

companion bill to the Brock amendment in the House. However, hearings were not held on the bill that Representative Heckler had introduced. Such hearings would have had to be convened by the Subcommittee on Consumer Affairs, whose Chairman was Leonor Sullivan (D–Mo.). Representative Sullivan opposed holding hearings at that time, and many leaders of women's groups felt that her resistance was due to her own lack of interest in feminist issues. (Sullivan, the only female member of Congress to vote against the ERA, however, claimed that she preferred to wait and draft more perfect legislation dealing with problems of credit discrimination against all groups.) In general, feminists distrusted Sullivan, who was viewed both as an anti-feminist and as a poor manager of bills.

The Second Round in Congress

The second session of the Ninety-Third Congress was convened in 1974. Senator Brock reintroduced his legislation as an amendment to the Federal Depositories Insurance Bill. The legislation that he chose to introduce in 1974 was stronger and more detailed than that passed in 1973, and was drafted in consultation with women's rights groups. By this time, business groups sought a more active role in the drafting of the bill, to make it one with which they could comply without great cost and constant danger of nuisance suits. Both industry and women's groups were represented at numerous consultations with legislators. Sharyn Campbell, by then an attorney for National Bank Americard, Inc., sought to wear "two hats" to help resolve conflicts between the credit industry and women. Like its predecessor, the 1974 bill that finally emerged, known as the Equal Credit Opportunity Act, had almost no opposition in the Senate. This time it passed the Senate 89 to 0. Both unanimous Senate votes in favor of equal credit opportunity indicate the perceived importance of this issue to congressmen's constituents, such that all senators wished to be recorded as having voted affirmatively.

Throughout the time that the legislation was being considered by the Senate, women's rights groups were active in encouraging support for its passage. (There was little doubt that the bill would pass the Senate, but there was concern that the House version of the bill might not even pass the hurdle of being considered in subcommittee—the subcommittee chaired by Representative Sullivan who had refused to hold hearings the previous year.) The groups that were most involved both in devising strategy and in lobbying for equal credit legislation during this phase of the legislative process included the NOW Task Force on Consumer Credit, WEAL, NWPC, and the Women's Lobby. Operating in the background as a source of technical expertise (as opposed to lobbying activity) was the Center for Women Policy Studies. Grassroots support in the form of letters and telephone calls, recruited in part from the membership lists of NOW, WEAL, and other groups, was also brought to bear on key subcommittee members. For example, the Washington office of the National Council of Jewish Women alerted all of its local offices so that women associated with the group would be advised to write letters and send telegrams to their senators and representatives in Congress. At this stage in the legislative process, many of the older and more traditional women's groups lent their support to the campaign for the ECOA by encouraging their members to get in touch with their representatives in Congress.

During the period immediately after the Senate passed S. 3492, the Equal Credit Opportunity Act of 1974, there was fear among many of its proponents that Representative Sullivan would not hold hearings on a credit bill. She claimed that if hearings were to be held on any bill, it would have to be an omnibus bill dealing with more than just sex and marital status—one including age, color, race, and national origin. Most women's groups felt that legislation of this type would take several years to be enacted, and that their immediate goal of ending credit discrimination on the basis of sex and marital status would thus be postponed. There was concern by women's groups, and by supportive members in the House of Representatives including Ed Koch (D–N.Y.) and Margaret Heckler (R–Mass.), that if hearings were not held prior to the end of the Ninety-Third Congress, a new Congress might not look as favorably upon anti-discrimination legislation, in part because of worsening economic conditions.

Under pressure from Koch, Heckler, and feminist groups, hearings were held by the Subcommittee on Consumer Affairs on two proposed bills dealing with credit discrimination: H. R. 14856, the bill introduced by Representative Sullivan (an omnibus anti-discrimination credit bill) and H.R. 14908, a bill introduced by Representative William Widnall (R–N.J.), which was directed to credit discrimination based on sex and marital status. Koch worked with feminist groups, the Republican minority staff of the Committee on Banking and Currency, and industry representatives to get consensus on a bill.

Prior to the House hearings and during the hearings themselves, women activists were involved in providing information to members of the House Subcommittee, and in trying to influence the outcome of the vote. Again representatives of the credit industry did not try to block legislation; they sought only to influence the substantive details of the final act. Many women's groups—the women's rights groups as well as some of the more traditional women's groups—testified at the Subcommittee hearings. Most of these groups used the research and arguments provided by CWPS, and many of the groups that presented testimony at the House hearings took essentially similar positions. Thus, in addition to testimony provided by Ann Scott of NOW, Patricia Massey of WEAL, Carole Burris of the Women's Lobby, and Margaret Gates and Nancy Polikoff of CWPS, testimony in support of legislation to end credit discrimination on the basis of sex and marital status came from groups as diverse as the American Association of University Women, the National Council of Jewish Women, and the National Federation of Business and Professional Women's Clubs, and from outside consumer groups that had been mobilized, most notably the Consumers Union.

This is not to suggest that women's groups were completely unified throughout the entire legislative process. Although they all agreed on the need for immediate legislation, NOW took what some viewed as a pro-industry position whereas other groups sought a more sweeping solution to problems of credit discrimination and enforcement. Among the latter were the Women's Lobby and NWPC, while Margaret Gates of CWPS, who also sought stronger provisions, was characterized by one observer as "taking a more radical view of a not-too-radical issue."

Points of contention included the strength of the class-action provision, the awarding of attorney's fees and court costs of successful plaintiffs, and the right of the plaintiff to recover under both state and federal law for the same violation. Additional differences existed regarding the mandatory disclosure by industry of reasons for denial of credit. The differences, however, did not weaken ultimate support for the passage of the ECOA.

Women's groups accepted an amendment to the bill (sponsored by Koch) that limited the amount of class-action recovery. Ultimately, the concession on the class-action issue was viewed by women involved as a *quid pro quo* for a broad definition of discrimination.

When the bill emerged from the House Subcommittee hearings and mark-up session, it was almost identical to the Senate-passed Brock bill supported by most of the leaders of the women's groups. This bill then went to the Committee on Banking and Currency for a vote. A legislative quirk occurred at about this time in the passage of the ECOA. The Senate passed the Equal Credit Opportunity Act (S. 3492) as well as a House-passed Omnibus Banking Bill (H.R. 11221). Senator Brock attached S. 3492 as Title 5 to H.R. 11221. The Senate was ready to go to conference committee on H.R. 11221. If a conference report were not issued, there could be no final vote in Congress and the bill would die with the end of the Ninety-Third Congress. Thus the House Committee on Banking and Currency assigned members of the Financial Institutions Subcommittee (that had originally considered H.R. 11221) to the conference. As a result, the credit discrimination amendment never reached the floor of the House for a vote, and the conference adopted a version of the bill similar to that passed in the Senate. The conference report (H. Rept. 93-1429) was filed on October 4, 1974, and approved by both Houses of Congress. The Senate approved the conference report by voice vote; the House of Representatives approved it by a vote of 355 to 1. The bill was signed into law by President Ford in October 1974, as the Equal Credit Opportunity Act of 1974. The main provisions of the law were to:

1. prohibit discrimination on the basis of sex or marital status, with respect to any aspect of a credit transaction (although inquiry of marital status is permissible if not used for discriminatory purposes);
2. provide for enforcement by thirteen relevant agencies of the federal government;
3. prohibit dual recovery at the state and federal levels; and
4. award punitive damages in individual suits of up to $10,000 and $100,000 or 10 percent of net worth—whichever is less—in class-action suits.

Credit was construed broadly to cover all aspects of credit extension by the retail industry, credit card companies, banking, home finance, and home mortgage lenders. The Federal Reserve Board was asked to prescribe regulations implementing the legislation before the effective date of the Act (October 1975), thus leaving some key issues to be resolved at the administrative level.

The efforts of women activists to direct congressional attention to the area of credit discrimination, act as informational consultants for congressmen, and play active roles both in presenting testimony and in sustaining legislative momentum resulted in a significant legislative victory for women. The passage of the ECOA suggests that although changes in popular views may be a necessary cause for changes in policy, pressure-group activities often must supply the sufficient cause. Far from being marginal to the legislative process (albeit inadequately financed), women's groups provided crucial informational resources and remained in close contact with Congress throughout. Their success may be contrasted with an account presented by Bauer, Pool, and Dexter, in which legislators characterized women lobbyists as "noble but impractical" and indicated that "the slightest questions on economic issues can embarrass them."[23]

Members of Congress were apparently sensitized to the credit issue and supported it overwhelmingly because they thought it had support of active women's groups in their constituencies. Women activists acted here as a vanguard, somewhat in anticipation of mass consciousness, prompting legislators to think in terms of "anticipated reactions" of female voters on this issue.[24]

The legislation as it emerged seems to fall into that category which James Q. Wilson calls policy with distributive costs and distributive effects that confers benefits on and spreads costs over a large number of persons.[25] While ultimately involving redistributive policy (for example, shifting social and economic resources to women in the long run and indirectly), this issue required no outlay of public funds and conformed to general standards of equity and fair play for women.

WOMEN AND THE FEDERAL RESERVE BOARD

The Administrative Process

The administrative system has been seen by numerous analysts as even more biased in favor of interests with money, technical expertise, and organization than the legislative system. According to Gary Orfield, disorganized groups lacking resources that wish fundamentally to alter the status quo face major difficulties in the administrative process. The civil rights

---

[23] Raymond Bauer, Louis A. Dexter, and Ithiel de Sola Pool, *Business and Public Policy* (New York: Atherton, 1963), 394-95.

[24] See *1974 Virginia Slims American Women's Opinion Poll*, Vol. III (New York: Roper, 1975).

[25] Wilson, *Political Organizations*, ch. 16.

forces he studied lacked professional and bureaucratic staff, established access, and centralized organization necessary to work out a consensus on questions of policy.[26] Women's groups shared these characteristics with civil rights organizations. However, the women's groups were conscious of the importance of the administrative process and, however intermittently, did intervene with impact in it. In contrast, according to Orfield[27] and Nadel,[28] for civil rights forces and consumer groups, legislation became an end in itself, and little attention was paid to the administrative process. Also, as suggested earlier, women had the advantage of technical expertise. Several capable women attorneys, who were expert in the credit area, were involved throughout the political process. In addition, and in contrast to the experience of civil rights forces in the Department of Health, Education, and Welfare and other administrative agencies, the staff of the Federal Reserve Board was uniquely sympathetic to women's aims. The feedback and encouragement of the Board's staff were often crucial to women's planning and strategy. Unlike the civil rights groups, the women's groups involved in the process of credit legislation and then administrative regulation were based in Washington and had numerous contacts with government due to their experiences with the passage of the ERA and other legislation. And although several active participants such as CWPS were prevented by 501(c)(3) status from playing an actively political role in Congress, they nonetheless were able to serve a catalytic function at the administrative level for other women's groups (administrative lobbying is not subject to IRS restrictions). Because, in Orfield's words, "administrative technicians are far more responsive to detailed, specific comments couched in the appropriate professional jargon,"

---

[26] Gary Orfield, "The Politics of Civil Rights Enforcement," in Michael P. Smith, ed., *Politics in America* (New York: Random House, 1974), 64-65.

[27] *Ibid.*, 65.

[28] Mark Nadel, *The Politics of Consumer Protection* (Indianapolis: Bobbs-Merrill, 1971), 170-72.

women who were able to supply this type of advice and criticism were in a relatively advantageous position.[29]

The Federal Reserve Board was given responsibility for establishing guidelines to implement the Equal Credit Opportunity Act. The Board has been viewed by some as a group of mandarins, isolated from public pressures but nonetheless subject to domination by monied interests—largely bankers and business groupings.[30] In recent years, the dominance by bankers on the Board has been lessened only by the inclusion of several economists. It was thus not surprising that, once the ECOA was signed into law by the President, business groups sought to use their influence at the Federal Reserve Board to obtain administrative regulations more favorable to their interests. What was more surprising was that they did not ultimately prevail, given what James Q. Wilson refers to as "bureaucratic clientelism"—"sets of established political relations that are extremely difficult to alter and tend to be self-perpetuating."[31]

Politics at the Federal Reserve Board

As noted previously, the Federal Reserve Board was charged with writing the regulations for the ECOA. A task force was appointed for this purpose, and it was headed by Lewis Goldfarb. According to a leading staff member, the staff was selected by the Board's most consumer-oriented member, Governor Jeffrey Bucher, who sought to change the Board's image with regard to emerging issues, such as consumer rights. Because the policy area was a new one for the Board, he sought to select a staff with a substantive background in consumer, civil, and women's rights who could help Board members to understand the complex issues involved in writing the new regulations (Reg. B). The task force took the unusual step of holding public hearings on the proposed regulations, which were scheduled to appear twice in draft form for public com-

[29] Orfield, *Congressional Power*, 19.
[30] *New York Times*, April 19, 1969, 59; Oct. 23, 1973, 70.
[31] Wilson, *Political Organizations*, 89.

ments and then in a completed form. This was the first time public hearings were held by the Board in the consumer area. The initial draft of the guidelines was issued on April 22, 1975. Public hearings on these regulations were held on May 28-29, 1975. Women's groups played a prominent role in testifying on the regulations; they also contributed extensive written comments. In addition, the task force contracted with CWPS for consulting purposes during the period of time that the guidelines were being developed. Hence women's groups—and especially CWPS—that lacked the extensive research facilities and trained lobbyists of business, but did have technical expertise, were able to provide significant input into the administrative process. The action of institutionalizing the inclusion of a newcomer to the political arena (and even compensating it!) was, to say the least, unusual and demonstrated the pro-feminist leanings of most task force members.

As the April regulations appeared, they were clearly sympathetic to women's groups. Among the provisions irksome to industry—and advocated by women—were the requirements that credit grantors preserve records for two years after a final action had been taken on a request for credit, that they maintain records of accounts in the names of both spouses retroactively, and that they furnish applicants whose credit was denied or terminated a written statement specifying why, if the applicant so requested.

Business opposition to the ECOA "regs" was reflected in an editorial from *Consumer Trends*, a business-oriented publication. The editorial referred to the proposed Reg. B as a "maze of legal booby traps" and called ECOA a "simplistic law" passed by "dishonest" sponsors and proponents. "The National Organization for Women and other elements of the Women's lib" movement have forced into Reg. B nearly every type of requirement or prohibition that they protested vigorously they were not seeking, the editorial contended.[32]

At the public hearings and in public testimony, a conflict

[32] *Consumer Trends*, May 16, 1975, 1.

in approach between NOW and the other women's groups became apparent, specifically over how far the guidelines should go in requiring mandatory disclosure of reasons for denial of credit, retroactive recordkeeping in husband's and wife's names, and the like. Susan Onaitis, at this time heading NOW's National Credit Task Force, appeared to agree with industry spokesmen in decrying the probable costs for credit companies of reviewing all their files retroactively. Endorsing a compromise proposed providing for the listing of (old) accounts in both names only upon the borrowers' request, she indicated that women sought only equal, and not unfair, advantages from credit grantors. Under pressure from the other groups, NOW retracted what were viewed as conservative, pro-industry positions and submitted new testimony (on July 14) to the Board more in accord with "pro-feminist views."[33] This incident indicates the degree of communication and, ultimately, unity present in the women's coalition on these complex issues. Nonetheless, Onaitis's initial comments may have weakened the feminist cause in the drafting of the second set of regulations by giving an impression to the Reserve Board of Governors of divided feminist ranks.

At the Federal Reserve Board's public hearings, held on May 28-29, representatives of the banking, consumer finance, and retailing industries told the Federal Reserve Board Governors that some parts of the draft regulations would be an "operational nightmare" and would require more paperwork and expense than the incidence of sex discrimination warranted. Spokesmen from Sears and the American Bankers Association decried the cost of millions of dollars necessary to provide written notice to unsuccessful applicants and carry accounts in names of both spouses, and they contended that the new rules would force small merchants to abandon credit plans, in favor of "impersonal" business by mail that would deny credit to many.[34]

[33] See the *Washington Post*, May 29, 1975, D7.
[34] *Wall Street Journal*, May 30, 1975, 2.

Business groups made a concerted effort to rectify what they viewed as an imbalance in the Board's first draft regulations; and the second set of proposals, issued in September, emerged as far more favorable to the credit industry and its concerns. Women's groups were less vigilant with regard to the drafting procedure at this stage, and they were caught somewhat by surprise. A good index of the relative concerns of the credit industry and women's groups can be seen in noting the mail responses after each set of draft regulations was issued. After the April draft (viewed as pro-women), of the 467 letters received by the Board, 310 were from business-related groupings and only 91 were from consumer interests. After the September draft (viewed as pro-business), of 420 comments, 191 were from consumer groups or individuals and another 64 were from government sources—many of the latter sympathetic to the feminist point of view.[35]

Immediately upon the issuance of the second set of regulations, women activists swung into action, seeking to mobilize the press, other media, and congressional sympathizers. Television newscasters were approached (primarily by Linda Cohen, Chairperson of the NOW Credit Task Force in Washington, D.C.) and stories were written on the need for affirmative action against credit discrimination. Eileen Shanahan of the *New York Times* and Sara Fritz of UPI wrote several stories sympathetic to the women's point of view. An outraged telegram from Karen DeCrow (President of NOW) to Chairman Arthur Burns of the Federal Reserve Board of Governors, and letters sent to all congresswomen and other members of Congress on relevant banking committees, denounced a "sell-out to the banking hierarchy" and betrayal both of women and congressional intent.[36] The letter to representatives and senators urged prompt comment to the Board of Governors. DeCrow demanded a meeting with the Board of Governors in order to present her views to them personally.

[35] Data made available to the authors by the Federal Reserve Board.

[36] These letters made available to the authors by the NOW Task Force on Credit.

At the same time, Representative Bella Abzug requested a meeting with Chairman Burns. She led a delegation of a dozen women congressional representatives to a meeting with Chairman Burns, Governor Jeffrey Bucher (the Federal Reserve Board member most responsible for the regulations and also the most sympathetic to the feminist view), and Janette Hart and Fred Solomon (Deputy Director and Director, respectively) of the Office of Saver and Consumer Affairs of the Board—the office responsible for the preparation of the credit regulations. At the meeting held on September 17, Federal Reserve officials pledged to rewrite provisions of the regulations (1) regarding income from part-time employment (to be allowed in considering credit worthiness), (2) clarifying a ban on all questions about childbearing intentions of credit applicants, and (3) regarding business loans (to prevent creditors from requiring a co-signature on such applications).[37] Women also protested the new regulations' postponement of the effective date of many aspects of the law and the absence from the proposals of a mandatory statement from creditors providing reasons for the denial of credit.

Pressure was kept up on other fronts. Linda Cohen of NOW established contact with Senator William Proxmire, Chairman of the Senate Banking Committee, and gained his limited support. The National Committee on International Women's Year was mobilized, including Senator Birch Bayh, its Enforcement Subcommittee Chairman. They, as well as Emily Taylor of the Interstate Association of Commissions on the Status of Women, Barbara Bergmann, Director of the Economics of Discrimination Project at the University of Maryland, and Dorothy Haener of United Auto Workers supplied written or oral comments to the Board of Governors, which may have had some impact. Under the aegis of Representative Abzug, a letter from nine women representatives to the Board of Governors made detailed and thoughtful comments on the

[37] *New York Times*, Sept. 19, 1975, 1.

defects of the September draft.[38] The Washington Council of Women Businessowners was especially forceful in pressing arguments advocating the extension of the regulations to many aspects of business loans.

The Board of Governors, clearly astounded at the furor from groups they had thought dormant, was forced to enlarge its domain to include new groups customarily not part of its constituency. The Governors found themselves ill at ease in an issue area far removed from macroeconomics and monetary policy—one in which time was short, the mandate broad, the statute often vague, and the field without precedent. The Board, therefore, sought to play a balancing role, remaining sympathetic to its normal constituencies' anxieties about costs and language, while trying to meet some of the demands of feminist groups. Although the Board operates independently of the staff (whole provisions were rewritten by the Governors), the liberal, consumer-oriented, and pro-feminist character of the staff did serve to provide women's groups with feedback and information that aided in formulation of an effective strategy.

The Outcome

The final regulations, issued by the Federal Reserve Board on October 16, 1975, represented a compromise between the demands of women and creditors. Women activists did achieve a major political success in sustaining their original goal of meaningful credit reform, but the final draft did not constitute a total return to the strongly pro-feminist language of the original April draft—even though there were fewer concessions made to the credit industry in it. Feminist groups won a provision stating that creditors must explain (not necessarily in writing) their reasons for denying or terminating credit to any applicant if the applicant so requests. Although the inclusion of this provision "represented a victory for feminist

---

[38] This letter was sent on September 25, 1975; Congresswoman Elizabeth Holtzman also supplied an independent and informed set of comments.

groups, particularly the National Organization for Women which had protested the absence of such a requirement in an earlier draft of the regulations," the victory was only partial.[39] Feminist groups felt that, without written statements from creditors, the law could not be enforced, and they were particularly concerned because creditors are not required to inform applicants about the right to such a statement.[40] Although the Board dropped the written notice provision as too heavy a burden on creditors, the regulations do specify a standard form on which creditors can check off reasons for denial. Several other important provisions, which had been fought over by women's groups and creditors, are summarized below. Women activists "won" on several key points:

1. Beginning November 1, 1976, new credit accounts used by husband and wife were to be carried in both names and reported to credit bureaus in both names. This provision permits women to establish a credit history.
2. By February 1, 1977, married couples who had previous accounts were to be informed by creditors that they may have the accounts carried in both names. In addition, as of June 30, 1976, notice of the Equal Credit Opportunity Act's ban on credit discrimination was to be sent to each credit applicant, together with the name of the relevant agency enforcing compliance.
3. Lenders are prohibited from inquiring as to birth control practices or childbearing intentions. This provision represents a stronger pro-feminist view than the September draft.

[39] *New York Times*, Oct. 17, 1975, 1.

[40] Amendments to the Equal Credit Opportunity Act, passed by Congress on March 12, 1976, require all creditors to provide unsuccessful credit applicants with written reasons for credit denial and strengthen other provisions as well (including punitive damages in class-action suits) initially sought by feminists in the legislative process.

4. A lender cannot refuse to open a married woman's account in a hyphenated form or form including maiden and married name.
5. A lender will not be permitted to discount income from part-time jobs, although such income may be evaluated to determine its "probable continuity."
6. Inquiries regarding the income and credit history of a spouse or former spouse are banned if such income is not to be relied upon as establishing credit worthiness.
7. Credit may not be terminated after a change in the applicant's marital status unless there is evidence of a new unwillingness or inability to pay. And, although a creditor may inquire and consider information on alimony, child support, or maintenance payments, if a credit applicant does not choose to rely on such payments to obtain credit, support income from them need not be disclosed. These provisions were eagerly sought by feminist groups.
8. Separate credit may be extended to spouses if each so requests and each qualifies for credit.

But female applicants for business loans would have more limited protection than borrowers of personal goods and services. Business credit would be exempt from the prohibition against inquiry into marital status, the mandatory record-keeping provisions, and the requirement on informational notice. Also, women had wanted unmarried people to be able to open joint accounts, but they lost on this issue. Another key point represented a compromise: creditors were required under the revised regulations to keep credit application records for fifteen months after final action. The credit industry had wanted a one-year retention period; the feminist groups, two years.

However, as a result of amendments to Reg. B (12 CFR 202) passed in Congress in 1976, effective March 23, 1977, several of the original compromises that were accepted by

women were modified to comply with the original demands
of the feminist lobbyists. Amended Reg. B specifies that notice
of an adverse credit decision must be given to the applicant
with the written reasons or a notice of the applicant's right
to written reasons within thirty days. Reg. B also establishes
a higher level of liability for punitive damages at the lesser of
$500,000 or 1 percent of the creditor's net worth in class
actions. In addition, records are to be retained by creditors
for twenty-five months after action is taken. All of these modifications were consistent with the earlier preferences of most
of the women lobbyists.

ASSESSMENT

Potentially sweeping change was launched by the contribution
of women activists to the Equal Credit Opportunity Act, which
operating in a vacuum created new policy in an area potentially affecting millions of women. While women thus succeeded in broadening the political agenda, they did so only
by conforming to the system's mobilization of bias. The issue
was relatively noncontroversial, involving distributed costs
and distributed benefits; although business may incur greater
costs, they will be passed on indirectly to the consumer, and
large groups of both women and men may profit from the
extension, for example, of mortgage credit to a two-income
family. Issue demands were specific, and they challenged no
fundamental societal values. Though ultimately a role change
issue in the sense that economic power may be transferred to
women, this policy was perceived as one of *equity* or equal
rights and as such had no formal opposition. The issue did
not involve mass publics and was resolved at the leadership
level of politics. There was no national precedent to rely upon,
hence a "policy vacuum" developed that facilitated possibilities for innovation.

In contrast to some other feminist issues (such as abortion
reform and the Equal Rights Amendment), women presented
a united front with regard to equal credit opportunity. Their

broad-based coalition was bolstered by the presence of an ongoing "policy system," created in part by the battle for an Equal Rights Amendment, which included sympathetic members of Congress, their legislative aides, Federal Reserve Board staff and members, and the press. In addition, women were perceived as a significant "potential" interest group that might be mobilized to defeat recalcitrant legislators at the polls. Thus a multilevel and multifaceted coalition, whose strength rested upon the "anticipated reaction" of women voters, was crucial to success.

Women activists showed themselves ready to accept less than total feminist victory; women compromised in both their legislative demands and, later, in their regulatory demands.

POLICY IMPACT

The ultimate test of a policy's success is its impact on the public and the degree with which the spirit and letter of the new law are accepted. It should be noted that virtually all monitoring by feminist groups of equal credit ceased with the enactment of Reg. B and the amendments to it that were passed in 1976 (largely at the initiation of other disadvantaged groups). For example, the Center for Women Policy Studies, which played such a crucial role in providing background expertise for the issue's acceptance, has moved on to study other issues such as battered women and has been rebuffed in its efforts to obtain further funding to assess compliance with the ECOA. The League of Women Voters was alone in pursuing a case in the courts in a class-action suit against Central-Charge and Riggs National Bank. In the end, private counsel took over and the suit was ultimately dismissed for lack of statistical evidence determining a pattern of discrimination, although the individual plaintiff did gain relief.[41]

Public awareness of the ECOA is difficult to measure; the available evidence is somewhat contradictory, but appears to suggest that the Act has produced considerable change in credit

[41] Interview with Maureen Thornton of LWV, Oct. 25, 1979.

practices due to both public interest and creditors' compliance. A 1977 Consumer Credit Survey came too early after the Act's passage to measure public awareness and impact meaningfully; nonetheless, it did indicate limited awareness by respondents of credit discrimination based on sex and marital status (in contrast to the data reported by the Virginia Slims Poll cited earlier). The Federal Reserve Board has made the suggestion, based on previous experience with other credit laws, that public awareness of these laws tends to develop very slowly.[42] Nevertheless, a Federal Reserve Board survey in November 1977 of eight large creditors found that, of 48.5 million notices of rights to separate credit history for married customers mailed by the *seven* respondents, 5 million replies were received: 11 percent of the customers requested separate credit histories.[43] The survey also showed that the revised Reg. B, requiring creditors to inform rejected applicants of reasons for credit denial either initially or upon request, produced considerable change as well. According to the survey, "many of the rejected credit applicants who were initially given reasons for credit denial supplied additional information and a high proportion of these were then granted credit."[44] A 1978 survey by the Commercial Credit Corporation found that more than 80 percent of women surveyed had applied for credit in their own name in the past two years, and a majority of these indicated that they had "experienced problems"; 56 percent of those surveyed said that the ECOA had made it easier for women to obtain credit.[45] Most women who were turned

---

[42] Board of Governors of the Federal Reserve System, *Annual Report to Congress on the Equal Credit Opportunity Act for the Year 1978*, Feb. 1, 1979, 13.

[43] "Exercise of Consumer Rights under the Equal Credit Opportunity and Fair Credit Billing Acts," *Federal Reserve Bulletin*, May 1978, 363-64.

[44] *Ibid.*, 365-66.

[45] Commercial Credit Corporation Public Relations and Corporate Marketing Research Departments, *A Survey of Women and Credit: How They Use It and What They Think*, Aug./Sept. 1978. Of 2,080 women surveyed, the response rate was 33.3 percent.

down in their request for credit asked for a written explanation or reapplied and were later approved. The survey found that more women with family incomes of below $10,000 applied for credit than did women with incomes of over $15,000. The survey suggests, then, that the ECOA may have had a considerable impact on credit awareness and credit worthiness among women, even among lower-class women. A study of equal credit accessibility to mortgage funds by women conducted under the auspices of HUD from 1976 to 1978 found limited discrimination on the basis of sex or marital status of the applicant. This may be the result of compliance with the ECOA, although we lack complete information on cause/effect relationships.[46] More recently, a *New York Times* report on female home ownership found single women as purchasers of one-third of all condominiums and one-tenth of all homes sold in the United States in 1980, a transformation surely due in large measure to equal credit legislation.[47]

With regard to federal enforcement of the ECOA, reports reveal a relatively small number of complaints specifically dealing with discrimination based on sex or marital status. The 1978 Report of the Federal Reserve Board does indicate, however, that noncompliance with the Act rose substantially during 1978, but attributes the apparent rise to better staff training and enforcement techniques. One difficulty in the process of enforcement involves the absence of an "effects" test; that is, there is only a limited effort to take into account practices that may not be motivated by the intent of the creditor to discriminate but do have a discriminatory effect. The Federal Trade Commission, which responds to the largest number of consumer complaints under ECOA, did settle a $50,000 agreement in civil penalties against Bloomingdale's Department Store in an attempt viewed by the FTC as a warn-

[46] U.S. Department of Housing and Urban Development, Office of Policy Development and Research, "Equal Credit Opportunity: Accessibility to Mortgage Funds by Women and Minorities" (Summary of Results), May 1980.

[47] *New York Times*, April 23, 1981, 1.

ing to other companies that might be in violation of the ECOA. Under the direction of Lewis Goldfarb, who heads the Bureau of Consumer Protection at the FTC (and who was one of the ECOA's most fervent supporters in his position at the Federal Reserve Board during the writing of Reg. B), there is an attempt to enforce the law with vigor. The Department of Housing and Urban Development has a special program to educate consumers on equal access to mortgage credit and to study the ECOA's impact, while the Federal Reserve Board and other agencies have sought to educate the public as to their credit rights through the issuance of brochures and a film strip called "To Your Credit." In its 1978 Report, the Department of Justice suggested that firms with questionable credit policies change them quickly after complaints are filed or after enforcement agencies bring them to their attention. Another factor contributing to what appears to be low ECOA activity is the tendency of creditors to accept those applicants who complain—although this process may not necessarily result in abandonment of all illegal practices by creditors.[48]

CONCLUSION

The current status of the ECOA is fraught with several paradoxes. The number of complaints under the Act has fallen off, and there have been relatively few law suits since the enactment of the law. Is this relative dearth of activity due to compliance or to lack of public awareness? An attorney for the Office of Saver and Consumer Affairs of the Federal Reserve Board commented on the difficulty of proving discrimination under the law: in the absence of comparative data on the treatment of other consumers, it is difficult to establish discrimination.[49] Is the limited monitoring effort by feminist groups due to limited feedback, feminist preoccupation with

[48] The Attorney General's Report to Congress Pursuant to the ECOA Amendment of 1975, submitted Feb. 1, 1976, 6.

[49] Telephone interview with Delores Smith, Federal Reserve Board, April 28, 1980.

other issues, or to the Act's success? To what degree does the multiple enforcement structure of the Act reflect disparate policies between agencies that are often unresolved? While the ultimate impact of the ECOA remains to be seen, we can at least point to preliminary data suggesting both creditor and consumer awareness of the Act's importance.

CHAPTER 5

TITLE IX:
THE POLITICS OF
SEX DISCRIMINATION

INTRODUCTION

To change the society in which one lives it is first necessary to modify the belief system of the people living in that society. One institution for transforming belief systems is the school. Thus, to alter beliefs regarding equal opportunities for women, one available route is education. In the past decade two legislative forays into the schools by feminist groups interested in improving opportunities for women have been reasonably successful. In 1972 Title IX of the Education Amendments outlawed sex discrimination in elementary and secondary schools as well as in post-secondary institutions; and in 1974 the Women's Educational Equity Act (WEEA) was enacted, providing funds for research and development to undergird women's efforts toward gaining equality in education. No real conflict arose in regard to WEEA in either the legislative or the administrative arena. But controversy began to rage in response to Title IX as soon as the implications surfaced. In this chapter we consider the politics of Title IX. It will be shown that issue-specialization and coalition-development can balance a strong countermovement on an emotionally charged issue.

In July 1972 Congress passed and the President signed into law the Education Amendments of 1972. Included among these amendments was Title IX, a provision outlawing sex discrimination in education. Emulating the equal protection aspects of Title VI of the Civil Rights Act of 1964, Title IX states that "No person in the United States shall, on the basis of sex, be excluded from participation in, be denied the benefits of, or be subjected to discrimination under any education program or activity receiving federal financial assistance. . . ." The primary responsibility for drafting the regulations for the implementation of Title IX was assigned to the Department of Health, Education, and Welfare, where the staff of the Office of Civil Rights (OCR) was given the job of enforcing this new anti-sex-discrimination clause of the Education Act.

The passage of Title IX did not come about because of pressure from feminist groups; rather, this legislation may be largely attributed to the efforts of Congresswoman Edith Green and Senator Birch Bayh. Controversy and debate over the bill were centered on issues other than Title IX, and no organized constituency opposed its passage. However, when the full extent of the law was understood and the effect of specific implementing regulations comprehended, hard lines were drawn, especially by the male sports establishment and by its defenders in Congress, in efforts to diminish the impact of the 1972 Amendments. A coalition of women's groups—traditional and feminist—has to date been effective as a counterpoise to the forces opposed to Title IX by beating back challenges to the existing legislation in Congress and continuously seeking more vigorous regulations and implementation at the executive level. In fact, when new athletic guidelines were issued in December 1979, it was clear that the women's movement had been successful in holding the line on the intent of Title IX.

Major conflicts regarding Title IX have involved levels of enforcement by HEW and have often centered on the issue of sex equality in intercollegiate sports. To the extent that the feminists have been successful, they have been able to redefine the issues of equal educational opportunity—both in sports and in other educational activities—as issues of role equity as opposed to role change. Title IX falls somewhere between the poles, because while it involves equity, it deals with questions of privacy and potentially radical change in traditionally male-dominated areas of society. Ultimately, as Doris Burton has suggested, "The athletics issue may well mask a growing concern over changing sex roles and not a concern about the impact of Title IX on revenue-producing sports."[1]

Although Title IX was approved by Congress in 1972, it was not until 1975 that regulations for implementing the law were issued. Implementation has lagged and feminists have pressed their efforts at the legislative, judicial, and administrative levels of politics in order to prevent the demise of Title IX. It took until late 1979 to gain release from HEW of a "policy interpretation" largely dealing with intercollegiate athletics. Because the new rules are known as a "policy interpretation" rather than "regulations," they did not have to go to Congress for approval. A congressional debate might have proved lengthy and would have involved continued efforts to weaken Title IX, possibly resulting in the law's reconsideration and further delay of implementation. The "threat of females to participate in activities sacred to male machismo" has produced almost a decade of unrelenting pressure by feminists to end sex discrimination in athletics.[2]

In the pages that follow we will discuss first the conditions that women's groups have been trying to redress and then the legislative and administrative forces that affected the drafting and implementation of Title IX. We will also attend to the interplay of group activities throughout these processes. Finally, the specific role of women's groups in influencing policy will be assessed in an effort to show that they have used the

[1] Doris Jean Burton, "Sexual Equality Through Title IX: Potential vs. Performance" (paper presented at the Midwest Political Science Association convention, Chicago, April 19, 1979), 37.

[2] Harold Howe, "Sex, Sports and Discrimination," *Chronicle of Higher Education*, June 18, 1979, 72.

tools of the status quo to incrementally change that same status quo.

Much of the success of the women's movement has been in keeping the spirit of the law intact against the rather formidable male sports establishment and lackadaisical enforcement by the OCR. Feminists have been successful in holding the line thus far because they have organized a coalition focused exclusively on sex discrimination in education, have been relentless in maintaining pressure on this relatively narrow issue, have been vigilant in fending off challenges to Title IX, and have been willing to use a variety of strategies to realize their objectives.

Nonetheless, their job has not been easy. The values of members of Congress and administrators do not support vigorous enforcement of Title IX while opposition groups—especially the National Collegiate Athletic Association (NCAA)—with financial backing and legitimacy have mobilized to counter feminist efforts through intensive lobbying. The OCR record of enforcement in civil rights generally is at best a mixed one—complicated here by what Doris Burton describes as the numerous decision points through which Title IX and other federal programs must pass. Policy initiated by Congress goes to the OCR (which often must clarify and amplify), is then sent to regional offices, and finally to 16,000 school districts and 2,500 colleges.[3]

BACKGROUND

Education for women in American schools has been deemed by critics within the women's movement to be unequal to that provided men. In particular, educational opportunities for women have been seen as limited by educationally reinforced sex-role expectations regarding the proper role for women versus the proper role for men. Thus women have been steered

[3] Burton, "Sexual Equality," 34.

away from pursuing careers involving mathematics and science. Girls have been rewarded for academic and social do-
cility whereas boys have been encouraged to be aggressive and
inquisitive. Female students have been discouraged from seeking advanced professional training and, until the last decade,
qualified women were often denied admission to law schools,
medical schools, and other professional programs. Thus in
1960 women represented only 6 percent of the total medical
school enrollment. (By 1974 women made up 22 percent of
first-year medical school enrollment.)[4] Similarly, women were
often kept by lack of financial support from following their
studies toward the Ph.D. Until the 1970s most prestigious
business programs did not admit many women applicants to
their MBA programs. The number of women in traditionally
male-dominated vocational areas of trade, agriculture, tech-
nology, and industry remained low (5 percent in 1972). Career
opportunities having been limited in these ways, women in
1980 had yearly earnings that on the average were 59 percent
of men's.

In educational institutions, women are confined to lower-
level positions. A 1979 survey found that women held only
one of every ten administrative jobs in public elementary and
high schools, while women continue to receive fewer tenured
faculty positions at all educational institutions. A 1978 study
by the American Association of University Women found that,
in institutions of higher education, women have made no statistical gains on faculties and only slight gains in administrative positions even since the passage of Title IX.[5]

Equal athletic opportunity similarly has been denied female
students. Sports have traditionally been an area where the
stereotype of men as participants and women as cheerleaders

[4] John B. Parrish, "Women in Professional Training—An Update," *Monthly
Labor Review* 98 (Nov. 1975), 49-50.

[5] *On Campus with Women* 24 (Washington, D.C.: Association of American Colleges, Fall 1979), 4-5; PEER *Perspective* 5 (Sept. 1979), 3; *New York
Times*, April 8, 1978, 24.

or observers has been reinforced[6] (see Table 7). Women's athletics are always secondary to men's. In most schools, boys' teams are better funded and equipped, and boys have better practice facilities and more practice time. Coaches for male sports are better paid than their female counterparts, and in college and university communities, athletic recruitment and scholarship opportunities have been dominated by men. Athletic expectations have reflected a general societal view of women as passive, unskilled, and submissive. This, then, is the backdrop against which the politics of Title IX must be considered.

THE PASSAGE OF THE LAW

Title IX, as adopted by both houses of Congress and signed into law by the President, bans sex discrimination in education. Several interacting forces seem to have been responsible for the introduction of Title IX into the Education Amendments of 1972. By the late 1960s women on American college and university campuses had begun to recognize the discrimination that they were suffering. Perhaps this awareness was wrought in part by the ripple effects of the civil rights movement on potential women activists, by the emergence of an organized, albeit small, women's rights movement, by the wave of unmet rising expectations that had been fed by President Johnson's executive orders of 1965 and 1967, and by the various state meetings of commissions on the status of women. Also, in 1969, WEAL initiated its first sex-discrimination case against universities that made a clearly articulated statement about the status of women in educational institutions. Then, in 1970, Representative Edith Green (D-Ore.) held congressional hearings that addressed questions of discrimination against women in education. Two volumes of hearings were published, and she had 6,000 copies printed so as to provide

[6] U.S. Commission on Civil Rights, Hearing, July 9, 1978, testimony of Carole Mushier, President, AIAW, 96.

TABLE 7
Universities and Colleges Offering Sports Programs,
by Size and Availability of Football
(1973-74, 1977-78, 1978-79)*

FOUR-YEAR INSTITUTIONS							
		Women			Men		
Size of Institution		1973-74	1977-78	1978-79	1973-74	1977-78	1978-79
SMALL (1-1000)							
No football	(N=203)	0.7	2.3	2.7	3.5	4.2	4.0
Football	(N= 84)	1.4	3.6	4.2	7.3	7.4	7.3
Subtotal	(N=287)	0.9	2.7	3.1	4.6	5.1	5.0
MED-SMALL (1001-2000)							
No football	(N=151)	1.5	3.1	3.6	5.0	5.2	5.1
Football	(N=157)	2.3	4.8	5.0	8.6	8.8	8.7
Subtotal	(N=308)	1.9	4.0	4.3	6.8	7.0	7.0
MEDIUM (2001-5000)							
No football	(N=122)	1.7	3.7	4.1	5.8	6.7	6.6
Football	(N=154)	2.7	5.6	6.0	9.3	9.3	9.2
Subtotal	(N=276)	2.3	4.8	5.2	7.8	8.2	8.0
MED-LARGE (5001-10,000)							
No football	(N= 53)	3.1	5.9	6.2	8.3	8.0	7.7
Football	(N=117)	3.9	6.6	6.9	9.9	9.8	9.6
Subtotal	(N=170)	3.6	6.4	6.7	9.4	9.2	9.0
LARGE (10,001+)							
No football	(N= 22)	3.6	6.0	6.4	8.1	9.1	8.9
Football	(N=116)	6.5	8.5	8.6	11.0	10.6	10.7
Subtotal	(N=138)	6.0	8.1	8.2	10.6	10.4	10.4
SUBTOTAL							
No football	(N=551)	1.5	3.3	3.7	5.0	5.6	5.4
Football	(N=628)	3.4	5.9	6.2	9.3	9.3	9.2
TOTAL	(N=1179)	2.5	4.7	5.0	7.3	7.5	7.4
TWO-YEAR INSTITUTIONS							
No football	(N=616)	0.6	2.1	2.4	3.9	4.3	4.1
Football	(N=186)	1.9	4.3	4.7	7.9	8.3	8.1
TOTAL	(N=802)	0.9	2.6	2.9	4.8	5.2	5.0

Table 7 (cont.)

SOURCE: U.S. Commission on Civil Rights, *Comments on a Proposed Policy Interpretation of Title IX of the Education Amendments of 1972 (Revised)*, Sept. 10, 1979, 4-5.

* This table may be read as follows: In the 1978-79 season, small four-year colleges with enrollments of less than 1,000 students that do not offer football have a mean of 2.7 sports for women and 4.0 sports for men.

the widest possible distribution of the testimony. It is interesting to note that apparently *no* post-secondary institutions sent representatives to testify at these hearings. Two years later Representative Green introduced Title IX to the 1972 Education Amendments. She requested the women's groups *not* to testify in behalf of Title IX because she believed that if members of Congress were not aware of what was included in Title IX, they would simply vote for it without paying too much attention to its content or its ultimate implications. Women's organizations complied with Representative Green's request and they stayed away from the hearings.

Feminist goals were met in the early legislative encounters on Title IX. In part this was so because most attention was directed to the other titles of the Omnibus Education Amendments. Title IX was not a central issue for many members of Congress. It was only in the process of implementation, when the potential impact was more fully understood, that opposition to Title IX began to take shape.

LOBBYISTS FOR AND AGAINST THE REGULATIONS

The implementation of Title IX has been complicated by the passage of the 1974 Education Amendments, which included a provision giving Congress forty-five days to disapprove by concurrent resolution any administrative regulations regarding education if they are deemed to be inconsistent with congressional intent. It was especially in this context that conflict arose and strong counterpressures were mounted to the anti-sex-discrimination goals of the women's groups. The male sports establishment (most notably, the NCAA and other groups of coaches) lobbied to prevent what they saw as a potential erosion in their power if equal educational opportunity in athletics and organized sports in particular were provided to all students regardless of their sex.

Though feminist lobbying for equal credit opportunity met some opposition from business groups during the time when regulations were being written for the Equal Credit Opportunity Act, this countermovement was mild in contrast to what women activists encountered at the same stage with Title IX. In the latter case, social values intervened, as well as a strong and well-organized counterlobby, the NCAA. Feminists had to contend with the internalized values of presidents, Congressmen, and administrators. Nonetheless, Gary Orfield has written that the Office of Civil Rights was "confronted by an active, informed and insistent constituency of women's organizations, a constituency with organizational resources and political power far greater than those of minority groups, as evidenced by the way it transformed the usually invisible process of administrative rule making and then successfully beat down a challenge to the regulations on the floor of Congress." Despite efforts to weaken the athletic regulations from local officials and influential House members, mobilized women's groups quashed the rebellion.[7]

Some sixty groups have been participants in the Title IX forays. In addition to WEAL, NOW, NWPC, CLASP-WRP, and other feminist groups, more traditional organizations such as the LWV, the Association of American Colleges' Project on the Status and Education of Women, the AAUW, the ACE, the AAUP, and the Girl Scouts, to name but a few, have been involved. In 1974 these groups joined together to form the Education Task Force, which later changed its name to the National Coalition for Women and Girls in Education. This

[7] Gary Orfield, *Must We Bus?* (Washington, D.C.: Brookings Institution, 1978), 347.

organization started as an informal lunch group of seven or eight people and then expanded into a larger coalition. The participants have been concerned with a single issue—sex discrimination in education—and they have always attempted to iron out their own differences on issues as well as tactics prior to taking public positions so as to minimize public divisiveness. Participation is flexible: members need join only on those matters with which they agree. Perhaps most responsible for the National Coalition's inception was Bernice (Bunny) Sandler, who is with the Association of American Colleges' Project on the Status and Education of Women, which supplied both early moral and financial support for the coalition.

The National Coalition generally works in conjunction with the AIAW, which is also a member of the group. The AIAW, founded in 1971, is the leadership organization for women's intercollegiate programs, governing scholarships, athletic recruitment, and other regulations for women in sports for 916 member shcools. With the aid of its legal counsel, Margot Polivy, a Washington attorney and feminist activist, it has played a crucial role in the struggle for Title IX. In addition to the AIAW, SPRINT (a branch of the WEAL Fund that acts as a clearinghouse for sports-related information and case histories) and PEER (a branch of the NOW Legal Defense Fund that exclusively monitors Title IX) have occupied major roles in the National Coalition. Other active participants include Marcia Greenberger and Margaret Kohn (the latter for a long time the chair of the National Coalition's Task Force on Enforcement) of CLASP-WRP. They have been highly involved in the area of sex discrimination in education since they brought the *WEAL* v. *Califano*[8] suit in the mid-1970s.

Observers attribute the National Coalition's success to its definable issue area, sharing of power by constituent groups, and narrow range of influence. Resources are limited, and the organization's role is essentially to meet biweekly, discuss is-

[8] U.S. Dist. Ct. for D. of C., Civ. Act. no. 70-3095 (1977).

sues related to Title IX, and delineate positions on policy. Under these conditions, there is little usurpation of any individual group's power and influence.

As noted previously, the major opposition to feminist groups regarding Title IX was mounted by the men's athletic establishment. In particular, the NCAA and the leadership of some universities with major commitments to men's intercollegiate sports have been in the forefront of organized opposition. The major counterforce to feminist efforts has not been directed toward the end of funding for Title IX. Rather, the focus has been the exclusion of athletics from Title IX enforcement. The NCAA, like the AIAW, an organization of institutions, was initially slow to mobilize opposition through college presidents and coaches, but has now become more active, although it has not prevailed politically despite its growing clout.

The countermovement has sought to operate in a manner comparable to that of the feminist groups, although a spokesman for the NCAA claimed that his group was neither as organized nor as aggressive as the feminists in Washington. However, in that the countermovement represents the status quo by simply not responding too quickly to demands for change, it has been able to thwart full implementation. Also, many members of Congress as well as OCR officials, if not active supporters of the NCAA, are "closet supporters" and have not made vigorous efforts to bring about change. As recently as 1978 the AIAW issued data that showed wide discrepancies in per capita spending for athletics between men and women at comparable institutions. In NCAA Division I schools, the mean per capita expenditure for men was $5,257; the figure for women was $2,156 (see Table 8).

The NCAA is an organization of 726 member institutions. It has the capacity to raise the political and financial resources necessary for lengthy litigation. For example, in 1978 its revenues totalled $13.9 million, with self-generated revenues deriving from championship games, televised football, and the production of other television sports programs. The leaders

TABLE 8

Athletes, Budgets, and Per Capita Expenditures (PCE)
at AIAW and NCAA Colleges (1978)
(figures given are means)

Membership	Number of Athletes Men/Women	Men Total Budget	Men PCE	Women Total Budget	Women PCE	Difference between Total Budgets
All AIAW Colleges	238/102	$717,000	$3,013	$141,000	$1,382	− 80.3%
AIAW and NCAA						
NCAA Div. I	315/138	1,650,000	5,257	276,000	2,156	− 83.3
NCAA Div. II	222/105	418,000	1,883	120,000	1,143	− 71.3
NCAA Div. III	251/110	79,000	315	24,000	218	− 69.6
All NCAA	276/118	1,042,000	3,755	199,000	1,686	− 80.9

SOURCE: *AIAW Competitive Division Structure Implementation Study: Final Data Summary*, Association for Intercollegiate Athletics for Women, Fall 1978, Table XIV.

of major universities can be mobilized. Finally, and not to be overlooked, although societal values regarding the female role may be changing, changes in perception among men and women occur slowly. When women do not make demands for athletic participation, then opportunities are not provided. However, if opportunities are not provided, women will often not request them. Thus the men's athletic establishment and academic officials may maintain the status quo while insisting that there is no need to provide equity. As of 1978-79 the OCR reported that a total of 1,179 coeducational institutions provided an average of 5.0 sports for women and 7.4 for men (for two-year schools, the comparable figures were 2.9 for women and 5.0 for men).[9]

WRITING THE REGULATIONS

The Office of Civil Rights of the Department of Health, Education, and Welfare was, as noted previously, responsible

[9] U.S. Commission on Civil Rights, *Comments on a Proposed Policy Interpretation of Title IX of the Education Amendments of 1972 (Revised)*, Sept. 10, 1979, 2.

for drafting the regulations for Title IX. In July 1972, when the OCR staff began to consider this task, they had had only limited experience in enforcing anti-sex-discrimination regulations with regard to faculty and no experience with regard to students. In November of the same year the first draft of the regulations was published. It was a "cut-and-paste version of the existing regulation covering race discrimination under Title VI of the 1964 Civil Rights Act, after which Title IX was modeled."[10] The draft was very general and vague, and after it was reviewed by other officers in HEW and by the White House staff, strong pressure was brought to bear urging much greater specificity. The redrafting procedure was not given a very high priority within HEW—as was evidenced by the assignment of only two lawyers in the General Counsel's Office (who had other responsibilities as well) to work on Title IX.

While the administrative process was generating proposed regulations, Congress was still taking action on Title IX. In May 1974 Senator John R. Tower (R–Texas) introduced an amendment to the Education Amendments of 1974 that would have exempted revenue-producing intercollegiate sports from Title IX coverage. This amendment passed the Senate. Since this provision was not included in the House version of the education bill, the House-Senate Conference Committee was left to resolve this difference (and two hundred other differences in the bills, too): On June 18, 1974, HEW released the regulations to implement Title IX. They provided coverage for schools and colleges in admissions, treatment of students (in athletics as well as other areas), and employment. In July of 1974 the House-Senate Conference Committee rejected the Tower amendment and included substitute language proposed by Senator Jacob Javits (R–N.Y.) that "reasonable provisions" for female participation in intercollegiate athletic activities be provided by Title IX. This committee also proposed

---

[10] Andrew Fishel and Janice Pottker, *National Politics and Sex Discrimination in Education* (Lexington, Mass.: D.C. Heath, 1977), 106.

the provision for the review of regulations within forty-five days mentioned earlier.

Although women had won in the conference committee, their battles were not over. They were caught unaware when, in October 1974, Representative Marjorie Holt (R–Md.) introduced an amendment that would have barred HEW from gathering data on sex and race discrimination in educational institutions. She was assisted by Representative Green, who by this time was upset by the less than rigorous interpretation of Title IX provided by HEW. The amendment passed the House by a vote of 200 to 169. When it reached the Senate Appropriations Committee, women's groups and civil rights groups were able to influence the committee members and the amendment was defeated in committee. Coalition contacts on the Hill used prepared questions and comments to support Title IX. Regulations for Title IX remained a volatile issue; HEW received nearly ten thousand written comments. There was, however, no consensus among the letter-writers. In November of the same year the Holt amendment was reintroduced as an amendment to an HEW supplemental appropriation. It passed the House by a larger margin than it had in October and again was defeated in the Senate.

Pressure began to mount on Congress to exempt social fraternities and sororities from Title IX coverage. Senator Birch Bayh (D–Ind.) introduced an amendment to exempt such groups. The amendment was carefully worded so that honor societies, recreational groups, and professional societies were not exempted from coverage. Women's groups did not actively oppose this amendment because Bayh had been supportive of women's issues and it was clear that social sororities and fraternities were as "American as apple pie." Two events followed these forays. First, women's groups, angered that HEW was not enforcing Title IX, in November 1974 filed a suit in U.S. District Court in Washington, D.C., against HEW and the Department of Labor (*WEAL* v. *Weinberger*).[11] In addi-

[11] U.S. Dist. Ct. for D. of C., Civ. Act. no. 74-1720 (1974).

tion, in February 1975 the final regulations were sent to President Ford for his approval. They were sent with a memo. Both the regulations and the memo were secret. However, a source in HEW sent copies to a women's group leader, who in turn distributed copies to other women's organizational leaders. Because of this crucial disclosure, the exact nature of the regulations was known in advance of publication; the women's groups were aware of the weakened character of the regulations, and they could consider a strategy prior to their enactment. In particular, there was a provision that required a person complaining of sex discrimination to use the school's internal grievance procedure before HEW would act on the complaint. Eventually this provision was dropped from the regulations—a testament to the women activists' lobbying and monitoring efforts.

At the same time that the women's groups were involved in trying to change the proposed procedure they opposed, some members of Congress still were busy trying to restrict the scope of Title IX by law. Representative Robert Casey (D–Tex.) introduced an amendment to a supplemental appropriations bill that would have prohibited HEW from withholding federal money from schools not offering coeducational physical education. The House passed the amendment; the Senate did not approve it. Later in 1975 it went to a conference committee where this effort to weaken the law failed.

On July 2, 1975, the President signed the Title IX regulations, which were weaker than the original proposed regulations. However, a new problem arose for the women when, on the same day that the regulations were issued officially, HEW announced a proposed rule change that would have led to the consolidation of all statutory civil rights enforcement— including Title IX enforcement—thus potentially weakening the law. The rule passed in 1974 mandating a period of review lasting forty-five days meant that Title IX regulations were now up for congressional approval or disapproval.

Despite some disappointment with the final regulations, the

women's groups decided to lobby Congress to approve the regulations, since there was some fear that if Congress disapproved, schools might take it as a mandate to continue sex discrimination. The regulations were sent to the House Post-Secondary Education Committee chaired by Representative James O'Hara (D–Mich.). O'Hara introduced a disapproving resolution and an amendment to "railroad" it through his subcommittee without hearings and thus with considerable speed; the full House Education and Labor Committee rejected both measures. Women's groups worked hard—with the support of women congressional staffers—to defeat the proposals. On July 21, 1975, three years after the initial legislation was passed, the regulations to implement Title IX went into effect.

But the battle was not over. The 1976 education appropriations measure was to become the target of congressional forces opposed to Title IX. Casey's amendment (to prohibit HEW from withholding funds from schools not in compliance) was again introduced. The House barely accepted it by a vote of 212 to 211; the Senate rejected the amendment 65 to 29. The Senate would not budge from its position. The House leadership finally threw its support behind deletion of the Casey amendment, and it was rejected 215 to 178 in a later vote. In this fight women organized their most extensive lobbying effort ever on any congressional issue, with hundreds of volunteers working under the guidance of the various involved groups.

The opposition to Title IX has continued even after these defeats, but the regulations have remained relatively intact. Although HEW withdrew its proposal to consolidate civil rights enforcement, to date there has been little actual enforcement of Title IX by the Office of Civil Rights.

IMPLEMENTATION OF THE LAW AND ITS REGULATIONS

As noted previously, the primary, though not total, responsibility for the federal role in implementing Title IX rested with the OCR in HEW. (When a separate Department of Education was established in 1980, the responsibility for Title IX moved with the OCR to the new department.) Insofar as the major federal responsibility for Title IX was granted to the OCR, only the role of that agency will be considered in this discussion of the federal administration of the law.[12]

It is important to recognize that ultimately all implementation of this law resides with school districts and college and university officers. The actual effect of the law will therefore be determined to a significant degree by the willingness of local officials to act in accord with the spirit as well as the letter of the law. It is well known that there is always significant variation in effects of a law when it reaches grassroots administration.[13] In the following pages, however, this phase of implementation will be given only cursory examination. We will focus our attention mainly on implementation at the federal level through the OCR.

The Office of Civil Rights must address two types of problems regarding implementation of laws: one is compliance and enforcement, and the other is policy. It is organized to take this division into account. The OCR is charged with the implementation not only of Title IX, however, but also of a variety of other civil rights and affirmative action policies. Its multiple responsibilities have tended to retard the OCR's effective implementation of Title IX policy. It was estimated by Cindy Brown, then Deputy Director for Compliance and Enforcement of the OCR (and previously a member of the Coalition for Women and Girls in Education), that only between one-third and one-half of staff time at the OCR was spent on cases of sex discrimination. The OCR office has had a poor record in civil rights enforcement in general. With regard to

[12] A good discussion for the role of other government agencies in the administration of Title IX is Nancy J. Balles, *The Unenforced Law: Title IX Activity by Federal Agencies Other than HEW* (Washington, D.C.: The National Advisory Council of Women's Educational Programs, 1978).

[13] George E. Hale and Marian Lief Palley, "Federal Grants to the States—Who Governs?" *Administration and Society* 2 (May 1979).

Title IX there has been limited coordination between the federal and regional offices, poor (almost nonexistent) record-keeping, turnover of personnel, and continual reorganization. According to Gary Orfield, the Title IX responsibility "was an extremely complex one for which few additional resources were provided."[14] (The 1975 regulations took up seventeen pages of small print in the code.) In addition, implementation of Title IX was complicated by disagreement among those people in the OCR charged with enforcement and compliance on just what the appropriate policy should be. There was limited interest by successive Secretaries of HEW in seeing the law administered effectively; hence no clear sense of priorities or mission was established. Furthermore, the OCR staff had more concern and involvement with implementing civil rights legislation as its affects nonwhites than with alleviating sex discrimination. The OCR staff in the 1970s was largely drawn from the black civil rights movement of the 1960s. In addition, it was mostly male, and seemed to be in questionable sympathy with the goals of women activists.

Despite these obvious roadblocks to active enforcement of the law, women's groups have remained vigilant—as have groups in opposition to Title IX—in monitoring the effects on Title IX. In fact, given the counterforces they must face, they have been remarkably agile in not losing ground. As noted previously, the major visible attacks on Title IX have been made by the male sports establishment, particularly the NCAA. The supporters of men's athletics have been successful in keeping equality of opportunity for women in sports as guaranteed in 1972 by Title IX from becoming a total reality. This is especially true in colleges and universities with NCAA Division I teams, somewhat less true in colleges and universities with NCAA Divisions II and III teams and in high schools. In 1978 only 13 percent of what was spent on men's intercollegiate sports was spent on women's intercollegiate athlet-

[14] Orfield, *Must We Bus?*, 307.

ics, although this amount had risen from 2 percent in 1974.[15] However, as compliance with Title IX regarding athletics increases in high schools, demands for better compliance in postsecondary institutions are likely to grow as well. In addition, as noted by an Assistant Deputy Director at the OCR, women's groups are rarely surprised by events since their representatives are always monitoring the system. Still, to date no funds have ever been cut off because of noncompliance with Title IX, and Title IX has not had the positive impact for which women activists hoped.

This fact, and the discussion of limited enforcement of the law, must *not* be taken, however, as indicative of either a total lack of effect of the anti-sex-discrimination provision of Title IX or of a failure by women activists in their continuing efforts to make Title IX's goals a full reality. It is essential to recall that success must be defined in terms of increments of change rather than total victory, although significant change may nevertheless be achieved. Also, though the sharpest attacks on Title IX are directed at equality in athletics, Title IX does affect many other aspects of the educational system. Admissions, course availability, student financial aid, counseling, housing and facilities, marital or parental status, scholarships, and employment practices all come under the purview of Title IX. Furthermore, sometimes changes have occurred in institutions because of multiple forces—internal pressures, influence of women activists, public opinion, the existence of Title IX—and not as a result of ongoing active enforcement by the OCR of the provisions of Title IX. Local-level monitoring by feminists, too, may make a difference in enforcement.[16] PEER's

[15] Interview with Margot Polivy, counsel to AIAW, June 20, 1978. By 1979 the figure was 16 percent. In Division I, with women comprising 29% of athletic participation, expenditures were 12%; Division II (32% women), expenditures 17%; Division III (30% women), expenditures 25%. Testimony, U.S. Civil Rights Commission, July 9, 1978, 98.

[16] June Petty, *Almost as Fairly: The First Year of Title IX Implementation in Six Southern States* (Atlanta: American Friends Service Committee, 1977).

guide to ending local educational sex bias, *Cracking the Glass Slipper*, is one effort in this direction.

The extent of federal enforcement was quite constrained during the first years of Title IX's existence. In 1977, at least in part as a response to the PEER report, *Stalled at the Start*, some efforts were made to invigorate enforcement of the anti-sex-discrimination provisions of Title IX. The PEER report was specific in documenting claims by the OCR that it was understaffed and thus unable to address all of the problems brought to its attention and in compiling data on the limited response of the OCR to complaints of sex discrimination. PEER reported that during the first four years of Title IX's existence

> 871 complaints about elementary and secondary schools were received by HEW. Of these, 13 were lost within the agency. The remaining 858 charged discrimination within the institutions of every one of the 50 states. . . . HEW managed to resolve just 179 complaints. . . . Two- and three-year delays were not uncommon. More than a third of the complaints filed during 1973 were still unresolved three years later. . . . In more than four years, the agency completed independent checks on just 12 of the nation's 16,000 school districts. There was no follow-up on information it collected in several nationwide surveys which showed Title IX violations. . . . [F]rom 1973 to 1976, HEW received fewer than two Title IX complaints against public schools each year for each investigator on the payroll. Out of those, the agency managed to resolve an average of three-tenths of one complaint per investigator. Even when the agency's other civil rights responsibilities are added in . . . the total case load of complaints filed

Despite a generally unfavorable picture, the author suggests that local-level monitoring does have some impact. A recent study of the Region X area makes similar points. See *Title IX Status in Region X: An Evaluation of Models and Barriers to Implementation of Title IX of the Educational Amendments of 1972, Government Region X of HEW* (Olympia, Wash.: Miller and Associates, 1978).

against public schools was just over six complaints per investigator each year.[17]

From the vantage point of what was gained from the investigations during the first four years of Title IX, the PEER report showed a rather dismal picture:

1. 18 of the nation's 16,000 school districts agreed to alter employment practices;
2. 21 districts agreed to upgrade sports programs;
3. 77 districts agreed to open traditionally male or female courses to both sexes;
4. 20 districts agreed to change sex-biased student rules; and
5. 21 institutions agreed to miscellaneous other changes included in the law.[18]

As of 1980 the OCR had attempted to cut off funds in only 33 cases, and in only a relatively few of these did the OCR press its charges to the hearing stage. A 1979 study by the U.S. Commission on Civil Rights found that enforcement was "unduly slow," data collected very incomplete, and information about discriminatory practices disseminated to schools by the OCR quite inadequate.[19]

FEMINIST TACTICS TO
MAINTAIN TITLE IX ENFORCEMENT

In addition to the issuance of *Stalled at the Start* by PEER, feminist groups also sought to keep pressure on the federal government through *The Unenforced Law: Title IX Activity by Federal Agencies Other than HEW*, issued by the National Advisory Council of Women's Educational Programs in 1978 under the Women's Educational Equity Act. This study provided careful documentation of feminist allegations and di-

[17] PEER, *Stalled at the Start* (Washington, D.C.: NOW-LDEF, 1977).
[18] *Ibid.*, 7.
[19] *Chronicle of Higher Education*, Dec. 8, 1980, 11-12.

rected public attention to nonenforcement. Feminists have continued pressure for more vigorous enforcement and strengthened regulations through other techniques as well. A quarterly newsletter published by SPRINT, *In the Running*, reports on the latest developments in athletic policy, while the *PEER Perspective* newsletter provides interested feminists with detailed analysis of Title IX legislative and administrative activity. Feminists have held demonstrations and a marathon track meet to dramatize their continuing commitment to demands for favorable Title IX policy. They have constantly pressed for meetings with HEW Secretaries (Richardson, Weinberger, Matthews, Califano, and Harris), OCR directors, and White House officials. For example, on June 20, 1978, representatives of feminist groups active in the National Coalition for Women and Girls in Education met with officials from the Department of Justice and HEW to discuss enforcement and better coordination between the two agencies. The National Coalition has also lobbied members of Congress repeatedly, urging defeat of amendments that would cripple Title IX.

To gain compliance with Title IX, feminist activists have had recourse to the courts as well. The WEAL Fund, in conjunction with other feminist groups, took legal action against HEW's record of noncompliance with Title IX. Through the consent order entered against HEW in December 1977 in *WEAL* v. *Califano* and *Adams* v. *Califano*, HEW promised to meet specific timetables and move vigorously against sex-discrimination complaints. HEW also promised to eliminate its massive backlog of 841 complaints by October 1979 as well as investigate 120 new sex-discrimination complaints in 1978. HEW was obliged to schedule reviews for assessing institutional compliance with the law and to issue computerized information reporting enforcement every six months. In July 1979 women's groups led by the WEAL Fund went back to court to charge that HEW had not fulfilled its obligation to clear the backlog, respond to new complaints, and schedule reviews for assessing institutional compliance.[20] Although Judge John Pratt failed to find HEW and the OCR in contempt, the suit may have succeeded in its aim indirectly, since the agency issued favorable guidelines on athletic policy within the year.

Feminists won a significant victory, also in the judicial arena, when the Supreme Court ruled 6-3 in May 1979 in *Cannon v. University of Chicago*[21] that Title IX permits individuals the right to file private lawsuits against educational institutions to enforce the law. Given the OCR's sporadic record in responding to individual complaints and its failure ever to cut off federal funds to recalcitrant institutions, this ruling provides an alternative mechanism for enforcing Title IX and strengthens the law. On the other hand, the Supreme Court has refused to review three lower court decisions holding that HEW does not have the authority to regulate employment practices under Title IX. This action leaves standing the lower court rulings that restrict Title IX's application to students only; the OCR has indicated that it would continue to investigate employment bias in certain circumstances. Thus judicial efforts have met with mixed success.[22]

Pressure from feminist groups has succeeded in gaining legitimacy in governmental circles for the National Coalition on Women and Girls in Education and the sixty-odd organizations it represents. Feminist groups have gained access to the policy-making structure in Congress and to the OCR, although their legitimacy as a pressure group does not always guarantee a totally favorable outcome. When Cindy Brown was Deputy Director for Compliance and Enforcement of the OCR, she was representative of a new feminist influence within the policy-making structure. On the task force responsible for HEW's December 1978 policy interpretation of Title IX and athletics (to be discussed below) were two women sympathetic

[20] *Ibid.*, July 16, 1979, 7.
[21] 441 U.S. 677.
[22] *Chronicle of Higher Education*, Dec. 3, 1979, 15.

to the feminist movement, athletic directors Diane Wendt of the University of Colorado and Christine Grant of the University of Iowa. PEER was asked to help improve data collection and monitoring at HEW. Formal and informal associations within a feminist network, both on Capitol Hill and in HEW, that involve officeholders and staff have helped to supply information and assess impact on Title IX. Feminist activists indicate that they are approached frequently for information on Title IX, a significant measure of their credibility at the federal level.

RECENT POLITICS OF TITLE IX

Largely because of *WEAL* v. *Califano*, there was some increased momentum in enforcing Title IX despite the continuing opposition of the male athletic establishment. According to Cindy Brown, more compliance officers were assigned within HEW to examine charges of sex discrimination in education. However, although the size of the agency's staff trebled (with 898 new positions) only one-third of the new staff members' time was devoted to work on Title IX issues. HEW threatened (but to date has not followed through with these threats) to cut off funds to several districts and institutions that were resisting compliance.[23]

Most recently the major focus on Title IX has centered on athletic policy guidelines, in order to clarify what was meant by "reasonable provisions" for female participation in intercollegiate athletics pursuant to the Javits amendment of 1974. An April 1978 memorandum made public a directive from HEW Secretary Califano that reaffirmed the applicability to revenue-producing intercollegiate athletics of Title IX. A task force appointed to draft further policy guidelines to aid in implementing Title IX's application to intercollegiate athletics was established, as noted above, with representatives of women's interests as well as with representatives of the educational

[23] *PEER Perspective* 4 (May 1978), 1.

establishment and men's athletics. Despite extensive lobbying by the NCAA, major revenue-producing sports were included within the guidelines, although several potential loopholes were left open. The draft guidelines issued in December 1978 provided that "substantially equal per capita expenditures" be made for men's and women's athletics, including such things as scholarships, travel, and equipment. However, "unequal spending could be permitted if 'nondiscriminatory factors' are involved, viewed by some feminists as a back door approach to excluding big time college football from the constraints of Title IX."[24] While feminists generally supported the policy, which provided for a (two-stage) immediate and long-term program to upgrade women's athletics, they saw the proposals as "overly ambiguous and not going far enough toward equality."[25] Nonetheless, an attorney for the NCAA characterized the policy as having been written by representatives of women's groups who had, in his view, "continuous and daily input." He also indicated his perception of the dominant presence of feminist groups in Washington—eight women to every NCAA spokesman. In his opinion, HEW staff members share the views and attitudes of the feminist lobbyists.

Although the guidelines sought to strike a balance between feminists and the NCAA, during the period allowed for public comment, which lasted until February 10, 800 letters opposing Title IX flooded both Congress and HEW. The NCAA again sought to have Title IX amended to exclude revenue-producing sports and established a coalition of 300 colleges and universities to modify or eliminate the proposed guidelines. A letter submitted to HEW from Terry Sanford, President of Duke University, and co-signed by presidents of several major college football powers called the equal per capita spending standard "anathema" and asked that each institution be permitted to develop its own nondiscrimination plan. Holly Knox, Director for PEER, retorted that this scheme was "little like

[24] *Chronicle of Higher Education*, Dec. 18, 1978, 9, and *PEER Perspective* 5 (May 1979), 1.
[25] *On Campus With Women* 23 (Spring 1979), 1.

asking the fox to come up with a plan for guarding the chickens."[26] Feminists countered the major university sports plan through a Coalition alert that sought to mobilize phone, mail, or personal visits to Congress to save the proposed policy interpretation. Female athletes and coaches who were often prevented from submitting comments through institutional pressure demonstrated and lobbied in Washington to influence Congress and HEW.[27]

Essentially feminists prevailed in their three goals: 1) to prevent Title IX from exempting revenue-producing sports, 2) to oppose riders to HEW's appropriations bill that would inhibit HEW's ability to enforce Title IX in athletics, and 3) to persuade Secretary Harris to release the final policy interpretation without submitting it to Congress for what might be weakening review.

The guidelines as finally issued in December 1979 call for colleges and universities to provide "proportionately equal" scholarships for men's and women's athletic programs. They must also offer "equivalent" benefits and opportunities in other aspects of intercollegiate sports. Secretary Harris appeared to strengthen the Department's resolve to enforce compliance when she released a list of 62 colleges which had not complied with sex-discrimination regulations. The feminist community was generally supportive of the policy interpretation, considerably different from the 1978 draft, while remaining vigilant regarding the actual process of implementation. The NCAA indicated it was "very concerned" about the standard requiring "proportionately equal amounts of financial assistance" to be made available to male and female athletes.[28] The NCAA's Executive Director, stating his concern with what he termed the new policy's "sex dictated quota system," predicted that a legal test would be sought.[29] Secretary Harris stressed the flexibility inherent in the new policy,

---

[26] *Chronicle of Higher Education*, June 18, 1979, 12.

[27] *Ibid.*, April 27, 1979, 19.

[28] *Ibid.*, Dec. 10, 1979, 1, 14.

[29] *New York Times*, Dec. 7, 1979, D19.

but promised that no sports, including those producing revenue, would be exempt. She indicated that 120 persons in the OCR would be responsible for enforcement, although ultimately the policy would come under the jurisdiction of the new Department of Education. Thus seven years after the initial passage of Title IX, clarification for the issue of athletics finally arrived.

In an earlier test of strength between the feminist movement and the NCAA, the politics of Title IX emerged at the United States Commission on Civil Rights as well as at HEW. The Commission held hearings in December 1978 on the Title IX proposals and urged HEW to exempt football from the requirement for equal spending, recommending instead a five-year "adjustment period" for equal football expenditures to be "phased in." Feminists countered by demanding a reanalysis and rehearing (held on July 9) of the Commission's findings. In a reversal of its earlier position, the Commission in September 1979 urged that colleges be asked immediately to equalize their expenditures on athletic programs for men and women and recommended the same to HEW. The reversal was hailed by feminist groups, which had lobbied hard for the rehearing and reconsideration, and denounced by the NCAA, in what had become a familiar political configuration.[30] Feminists were successful in gaining access and influence on this issue, a major priority for them.

The policy interpretation on athletics led to legal action by the NCAA, which contended that the new regulations were "arbitrary and capricious" and exceeded congressional intent. Now the NCAA appears to be seeking the demise of the women's athletic group, AIAW, by attempting to establish competing women's programs. Thus, if it cannot win the legal and political battles, the NCAA will try to "take over" the field of women's athletics.[31] The controversy regarding Title

[30] *Chronicle of Higher Education*, Sept. 17, 1979, 15.

[31] *On Campus With Women* 27 (Summer 1980), 3; *Chronicle of Higher Education*, Jan. 14, 1980, 1, 14.

IX and its precise meaning will therefore continue in several different arenas.

Conclusion

In the years since the initial enactment of Title IX of the Education Amendments of 1972, there have been many attempts to alter the intent of the law, both by amendment and by regulation. To date, most of the efforts have failed, though actual enforcement is clearly uneven. The role of women's groups in influencing the writing of regulations and enforcement of the law has been difficult because of the resistance stemming from the personal values of members of Congress and the bureaucracy (especially regarding sports) and the existence of organized counterpressures.

Feminists have used a variety of strategies including litigation, publicity, and monitoring in order to influence the policy-making process. Through the use of a highly effective coalition, the Coalition for Women and Girls in Education, they have shared information, effectively divided responsibility, and presented a united political front and the image of broad-based political support. The maintenance of this effective single-issue group, which draws on the resources of mass membership groups, specialized research and legal organizations, and staff and elected officeholders in federal office, has gained credibility for feminist interests in education. Feminists have gained access to the policy-making process both in Congress and in HEW. In Congress they have beaten back repeated efforts to weaken Title IX through riders and modified appropriations. At the Office of Civil Rights they were viewed as "the most assertive, viable, and well-organized group," according to one lone-time observer. They have gained a consulting role, have placed feminists in positions of influence within the agency, and have won access to Secretary Califano, and then to Secretary Harris, pressuring them to move toward issuance of long-desired rules clarifying the relationship between Title IX and intercollegiate athletics.

While most policy makers viewed the feminists as persuasive and often highly effective, this opinion is not universally shared by all the involved actors. One high-level HEW administrator referred to the feminist constituency as "the most vocal, not necessarily the most effective" group pressuring for policy change at the OCR. A member of the U.S. Commission on Civil Rights referred to the adversarial relationship feminists have had with the Commission; she commented that they did little to maintain ongoing relationships with the Commission's staff. (The reason may be the limited attention the Commission has paid to most women's issues and the feminists' need to conserve their resources and energy.) Another OCR policy administrator commented that "although feminists yell the loudest, Title IX is the worst enforced law." Nonetheless, he suggested that when feminists were successful, it was because they were good politicians who "understand, compromise— would help us as soon as beat us over the head." This policy maker also indicated that feminists were justified in their concern over the slowness with which the agency had dealt with policy implementation. In his view, although feminists sometimes squandered their resources on "unimportant" issues such as hair and dress codes, without them there would be no policy on athletics. He averred that feminist lobbying on Capitol Hill was particularly potent—"they came in with facts and neutralized the opposition effectively." At the administrative level, the use of the marathon track meet mentioned above and constant pressure on Secretary Califano led to a belated but ultimate acceptance not necessarily of feminist views but of their influence and tenacity.

The issue of athletics is one particularly challenging to values regarding the place of women in society and moves from the more easily resolved role equity issues to those of role change. Despite this characteristic, and the existence of formidable adversaries in the NCAA and among prominent college and university presidents, feminists have held their own. It should be noted that on several occasions—in 1975, when the regulations were reviewed by Congress, and in 1979, when the athletics guidelines representing a compromise between feminists and the athletic community were issued—women's groups have been in the position of defending policies with which they are not entirely comfortable. But they have felt that the realities of politics require a philosophy of pragmatism and have worked to gain acceptance for such policies.

Hence, despite efforts to stall enforcement of Title IX, especially regarding athletics, some substantial changes have taken place. Increasingly, women's sports are receiving additional institutional funding; scholarships are being made available to women athletes; more options in sports are open to women; and physical education classes are integrated. Because feminist groups have been united and have played by the "rules of the game," they have succeeded where a more shrill and less organized approach might have led to a different outcome. Furthermore, by constantly monitoring the political process, they have not been caught unaware when a new effort to water down the law or the regulations has been attempted. In the absence of feminist pressure, Congress would most probably have vitiated Title IX while HEW would have ignored it. The continuing dynamics of Title IX will focus on the strength of opposition groups, politics at the new Department of Education, problems of maintaining financial resources for feminist groups, and continuing efforts to monitor policy at the local as well as federal level.

CHAPTER 6

WOMEN DIVIDED AMONG THEMSELVES: "THE RIGHT TO LIFE" VERSUS "FREE CHOICE"

INTRODUCTION

More than any other area of policy considered here, the issue of free choice in abortion appears to involve questions of fundamental role change for women. Peter Skerry has argued that "the defense of traditional moral and sexual values underlies the resistance to abortion reform."[1] Abortion is seen as a technique for preventing or postponing families, hence as a threat to the traditional family structure. Others have found that anti-abortion attitudes are correlated with opposition to premarital sex, divorce, contraception, and sex education.[2] Thus the issue of women's control of their reproductive capacity appears to touch the core of sexual politics and to challenge basic values about appropriate sexual and social behavior. There appears to be a deep-seated anxiety about the consequences if and when women are freed from the restraints of biological motherhood.[3] The essence of power relationships in society may be at stake in the abortion issue.

[1] Peter Skerry, "The Class Conflict Over Abortion," *Public Interest* 52 (Summer 1978), 52, 70, 79.

[2] Donald Granberg, "Pro Life or Reflection of Conservative Ideology," *Sociology and Social Research* 62 (April 1978), 414-29.

[3] Barbara Hayler, "Abortion," *Signs* 5 (Winter, 1979), 322-23.

Background

Abortion was widely accepted in the United States until the middle of the nineteenth century. Prior to the nineteenth century the legal status of abortion followed the traditional British common law. For hundreds of years before 1800 the governing principle regarding abortion was tied to quickening. Quickening is the first sense of fetal movement felt by the mother. Such fetal movement usually occurs late in the fourth month or early in the fifth month of pregnancy. The common law did not recognize the existence of a fetus in criminal cases until such quickening had taken place. In addition, destruction of a fetus in the second half of a pregnancy was punished less harshly than the destruction of other human life. Before quickening the termination of a pregnancy was not considered criminal in England or the United States. The moral question whether or not a fetus is a living being had been debated for thousands of years. In fact, the British common law doctrine, tied as it was to the quickening doctrine, apparently arose out of the medieval disputes over whether an ovum possessed a soul.[4]

During the nineteenth century abortion began to be proscribed and punished by criminal law in virtually every state in the Union. Between 1821 and 1841 ten states and one territory enacted laws that made certain kinds of abortion violations of statutes, rather than leaving common law practice as the governing doctrine.[5] The trend to enact anti-abortion laws continued unabated until the end of the nineteenth century. The laws became harsher as the years wore on. Every state except Kentucky had an anti-abortion law by 1900. In Kentucky the state courts outlawed the practice.[6]

A recent analysis of these stringent anti-abortion laws suggests that the radical reversal of previous customs was linked in part to efforts by the "regular" physicians to regain control

[4] James Mohr, *Abortion in America 1800-1900* (New York: Oxford University Press, 1978), 3-4.
[5] *Ibid.*, 20.
[6] *Ibid.*, 229-30.

over medical practice and to nativist prejudice that feared the dominance of immigrant population in the absence of a prohibition against abortion. Hence criminal abortion statutes were not motivated primarily by concern for the physical dangers of abortion to women, despite rhetoric that sometimes emphasized such concern.[7]

Physicians dedicated to the principles of scientific medicine, known collectively as "regulars," tended to be graduates of the country's better medical schools or to follow the lead of those who were. As a group they believed in such principles as rational research and cooperative exchange of information. These regulars organized and maintained state and local medical societies, published journals, and worked to maintain high educational standards at the nation's medical schools. Other physicians, known as "irregulars," who were not committed to the same principles as the regulars, were entering the medical profession in unprecedented numbers. They were in competition with the regulars for patients. The regular physicians often were in moral opposition to abortion—related in part to their roles as "social and intellectual modernizers in a world that still took for granted the assumption that a widespread and routine destruction of life was part of the human condition," or perhaps their desire "to find secular absolutes to replace spiritual ones."[8] Furthermore, the regular physicians perceived that abortion was a medical procedure that gave their competition, the irregulars, a competitive edge and also undermined the unity of their own ranks. As more and more irregulars began to advertise their willingness to perform abortions, especially after 1840, the regulars began to grow more and more concerned about losing their practices. If a woman went to an irregular for an abortion, she might continue using that doctor for other medical needs, thus affecting the size of the clientele of the regular physicians over the long term.[9]

The regulars' triumph over their competition in getting re-

7 *Ibid.,* 255-56.
8 *Ibid.,* 36.
9 *Ibid.,* 36-38.

strictive legislation passed ushered in an era when abortions became increasingly difficult to obtain legally, an era that lasted until 1973. In that year, in its decision in *Roe* v. *Wade*,[10] the Supreme Court struck down restrictive anti-abortion laws in the United States. According to one analysis of the abortion struggle, "feminist organizations adopted the cause of abortion reform or repeal as a rallying point. In the social history of the movement, abortion may have been as significant a unifying goal . . . as the movement was to changing abortion attitudes."[11] In *Roe* v. *Wade* the Supreme Court held that the "right of privacy" includes the decision to have an abortion, but that the state's compelling interest in regulating abortion increased after the first trimester of pregnancy. The Court rejected the view that an unborn fetus has a constitutional "right to life."

The Court's decision effected nationwide changes of significant magnitude. In 1973 a total of 745,000 legal abortions were performed in the United States; by 1977 the number had grown to 1.3 million. However, it has been estimated that 600,000 women who wanted abortions in 1977 were still not able to obtain them. Poor women, teenagers, minority women, and rural women were most affected by the inaccessibility of abortion procedures due to distance, lack of funds, or lack of knowledge regarding availability.[12]

In response to the decision, two opposing trends emerged and soon came into direct conflict. The feminist movement through coalitions and other efforts coalesced behind the decision, and even groups such as WEAL that had initially opposed "free choice" for abortion rallied in support of this issue. At the same time the judicial decisions helped generate a vigorous organized opposition that sought legislative and constitutional amendments restricting access to abortion. These

[10] 410 U.S. 113.

[11] Malcolm Potts, Peter Diggory, and John Peel, *Abortion* (New York: Cambridge University Press, 1977), 357.

[12] *Abortions and the Poor: Private Morality, Public Responsibility* (New York: Alan Guttmacher Institute, 1979), 5.

efforts have continued and have limited implementation of the 1973 Court ruling, even leading to modifications of it. A highly mobilized anti-choice movement, which calls itself the "right-to-life" movement, with considerable grassroots support and the backing of the Catholic Church has been unremitting in its efforts to limit access to abortion in every way possible.

This is the context in which the politics of abortion must be considered: the expansion of conflict, changing societal values, highly mobilized supporters and opponents, and political activity relating to abortion at numerous points in the political process. Like Title IX, implementation of abortion reform involves activity at the federal level as well as local discretion.

This issue, unlike others examined in this study, pits women against one another. Powerful political symbols have been manipulated by both sides in the struggle to attempt to sway public opinion their way. Conflict has escalated, drawing larger numbers into active or peripheral participation. Succinctly, "pro-choice" activists may be said to hold the view that the reproductive decision is possibly the most important a woman can make; it is a fundamental issue of self-determination. In contrast to this position emphasizing *women's rights*, "right-to-life" activists are concerned with the *rights of the fetus*, whom they believe to have a soul and the same rights as any other human being. Although not all the political decision makers who have eroded the blanket *Roe* v. *Wade* pro-choice decision justify their positions in theological and moral terms, many do. The ideological underpinnings of the pro-life movement itself rest on theological and moral grounds. It is the belief of pro-lifers that life begins at conception and thus the aborting of a fetus is equivalent to murder. Most pro-choice supporters of the feminist movement adhere to the view that life begins with viability of a baby out of its mother's body and thus the termination of a pregnancy in the early months is not the ending of a human life. Advocates of free choice sometimes question at what point a fetus is viable, but most agree that this is reached in the last trimester. Medical opinion varies on the question of viability, though scientific support exists for the viability of a fetus out of the mother's womb in the last half of pregnancy.

In the remainder of this chapter the major actors—both in government and among interest groups—will be identified and analyzed. In addition, their interactions in coalitions and in strategies pursued will be examined in relation to legislative activity and judicial decisions. In particular, we will look closely at the political decision making surrounding the Hyde amendment to the HEW annual appropriation. Because of the role change aspects of "free choice," feminists have met stiffer opposition to their goals on this issue than they have on role equity issues. Increasingly, pro-choice forces have been forced to seek alternative routes to the legislative process. They have pursued legal strategies and have turned to grassroots organizing and active campaigning for pro-choice candidates for public office in order to recoup their earlier position that seemed so promising in 1973.

ABORTION POLITICS

The 1973 Supreme Court decision in *Roe* v. *Wade* was seen as a major advance in women's rights. However, in the aftermath of the decision, the right-to-life movement has worked to weaken its impact by influencing members of Congress to pursue legislative countermeasures. In addition to gaining passage of the Hyde amendment to the annual appropriations bill for HEW and the Labor Department, which restricts government funding of abortions for poor women, right-to-life strategists have sought to get anti-abortion amendments attached to many significant appropriation bills. This is a short-term tactic inasmuch as their long-term goal is to secure an anti-abortion amendment to the Constitution.

Though divided on specific aspects of the credit law, women's groups were all in agreement that a legislative solution was necessary in order to eliminate credit discrimination against women. No strong counterpressures to the intent of a law were generated, and no strong moral or cultural opposition to equal credit existed. In fact, equal credit was a reasonably clear case of a demand for role equity and thus easily gained legitimacy. In contrast, feminist activists have confronted strong countermobilization on the issue of "free choice" and have emerged with varying degrees of success.

Since 1974, in an attempt to limit the impact of *Roe* v. *Wade*, which denied states the right to interfere with a woman's decision to have an abortion during the first trimester of pregnancy, Representative Henry J. Hyde (R–Ill.) annually has introduced an amendment to the appropriations bill for HEW and Labor banning the use of Medicaid funds to pay for abortions. The original Hyde amendment essentially denied Medicaid funding for abortion except in very restrictive circumstances (1) where the mother's life is endangered, (2) where she would suffer "severe and long-lasting health damage" as certified by two physicians, and (3) where pregnancy is due to rape or incest as reported promptly to a law enforcement agency or public health service.

Congressional debate has centered on the language of the amendment, with feminists seeking the vaguest language possible and right-to-life advocates striving to obtain the most restrictive wording possible—abortion only when the mother's life is endangered. During the annual confrontation the House has proven to be more prone to accept anti-abortion appeals while the Senate until 1979 held out for a pro-choice perspective. The inconsistencies between bills passed by the two houses were resolved by conference committee. In 1974 and 1975 the Congress failed to approve the Hyde amendment. In 1976 the House easily approved the amendment, but the Senate refused to ban federal funding of abortions for the poor. On August 25, 1976, the Senate voted 35-53 to reject the Hyde amendment and sent it back to the conference committee, where the Senate conferees had previously compromised and accepted it. Senators Birch Bayh (D–Ind.), Edward Brooke (R–Mass.), and Robert Packwood (R–Ore.) led the "free choice" forces in the Senate, which were adamant in their pro-choice position, while in the House support for the

Hyde amendment was increasing. As a result, conferees from each house were locked into their differing positions on the issue. Representative Silvio Conte (R–Mass.) offered a compromise proposal that finally proved acceptable to the conferees. The substitute amendment barred the use of federal funds to pay for abortions "except where the life of the mother would be endangered if the fetus were carried to term." The language used was intentionally vague, and Conte was quoted as saying that "it will be up to HEW to interpret this." The appropriations bill with the modified Hyde amendment was approved by both houses of Congress and was sent to President Ford for his signature. The President vetoed the bill. At that time liberals were placed in the uncomfortable position of wanting to vote to override the veto because of the funding for human resource needs that were included in the bill. Members of Congress who were opposed to the Hyde amendment, such as Representative Bella Abzug (D–N.Y.), who called the anti-choice amendment "unconstitutional, illegal and discriminating," felt obligated to vote to override because they supported the spending levels in the bill. The House voted to override the veto by a vote of 312 to 93. The Senate followed suit with a vote of 67 to 15. The ban on the use of federal funds to pay for abortions thus became law in part as a result of votes by liberal, pro-choice members of Congress.[13]

Additional review of this issue is useful in order to understand the problems women confronted in this area. The ban was enacted into law for FY 1977; however, it was not implemented at that time because a federal injunction, resulting from a legal challenge, was initiated in the Federal District Court for the Eastern District of New York. In fact, the pro-choice groups under the direction of the National Abortion Rights Action League had laid plans for a court test of the modified version of the Hyde amendment as soon as the bill became law, and both they and their congressional allies were

[13] *Congressional Quarterly 1976 Almanac* (Washington, D.C.: Congressional Quarterly, 1976), 802-804.

less insistent on a favorable bill for FY 1977 because of their certainty of reversal in the Supreme Court.[14] To the surprise and chagrin of women activists, the Supreme Court ruled on June 20, 1977, in *Maher* v. *Roe*[15] that it is not a violation of constitutional "equal protection" for a state participating in a Medicaid program to refuse to pay expenses incident to nontherapeutic abortions. A second decision, *Beal* v. *Doe*,[16] found that exclusion of nontherapeutic abortions under Title XIX of the Social Security Act (Medicaid) was not "unreasonable."

Subsequent legislative debate in the summer and autumn of 1977 dealt primarily with the issue of whether Congress would vote an absolute ban on use of federal funds for all Medicaid abortions or whether language adopted in the Senate on June 30, 1977, to ban federal funds except when the mother's life is in danger, when the cause of pregnancy is rape or incest, or when it is considered "medically necessary" would prevail. On December 7, 1977, a partial ban was approved and written into the law, when the House of Representatives finally approved compromise language by a vote of 191 to 167. The FY 1978 amendment provided for federally funded abortions if the mother would suffer "severe and long-lasting health damage" in the event of the birth, and also provided for the funding of "medical procedures" in cases of rape or incest promptly reported to relevant law enforcement or health authorities. The Secretary of HEW was instructed to promulgate directives for implementation.[17]

Joseph Califano, Secretary of HEW during the early years of Jimmy Carter's presidency, was, like the President himself, firmly opposed to free choice. (It should be noted here that President Carter, though opposed to abortion, never favored a constitutional amendment to ban it.) Although HEW sta-

[14] *New York Times*, June 2, 1977, 22; *Congressional Quarterly 1976 Almanac, ibid.*

[15] 97 S. Ct. 2376.

[16] 97 S. Ct. 2366.

[17] *New York Times*, Dec. 8, 1977, 1.

tistics showed that, as a result of the initial Hyde amendments and the implementing regulations, Medicaid abortions had decreased by about 98 percent in 21 states, Califano approved amended regulations effective August 1978 that further tightened the implementation of the Hyde amendment. The amended regulations require a victim of rape or incest who seeks an abortion to disclose her address, the date of the incident, and the date of the report. If another person reports the incident, he or she must give a name and address. The initial regulations required only the name of the victim. NARAL leadership feared that the changed regulations would pose a question of privacy for the woman and would make it more difficult for a woman to report such a crime when her address would become known to law enforcement officials and the press. Also, physicians certifying severe and long-lasting physical damage must include the patient's address. The two physicians who certify such "damage" must, moreover, be "financially independent" of each other; that is, the income of more than one of the doctors must not be affected by the abortion fee.[18] These regulations have remained in place for all subsequent Hyde amendments. The pro-choice coalition was unable to effect any loosening of the regulations during Califano's tenure at HEW.

The pro-choice groups continued to lobby on the Hill for an end to subsequent Hyde amendments or at least for a loosening of the anti-choice language. But the 1977 experience was repeated in both 1978 for the fiscal 1979 budget and in 1979 for the fiscal 1980 budget, though the results for the pro-choice coalition were considerably more devastating for fiscal 1980 than they had been in the earlier years. On June 27, 1979, Representative David Obey (D–Wis.) introduced an amendment in the House of Representatives that would have continued the Medicaid funding restrictions that had been law for the prior two fiscal years. The amendment was defeated 241-180 because anti-choice forces argued that the

[18] *NARAL Newsletter* 10 (Aug.-Sept. 1978), 1.

language was "too liberal" and was tantamount to providing "abortion on demand." On July 27, 1979, the Senate voted 57-42 to continue to use the language of the existing amendment (that is, the same language as the Obey amendment).[19] This was a weakening of the Senate position of previous years when they had supported funding for all "medically necessary" abortions. Next, when the House of Representatives voted out its version of the HEW-Labor appropriations bill, it included an amendment that would have funded abortions only when the life of the mother is endangered. The Senate, as just noted, in its version of the appropriations bill included the less restrictive amendment. The Senate and House conferees could not reach any mutually acceptable position on the abortion amendment, and thus in FY 1980 the Departments of HEW and Labor were funded under a continuing appropriations resolution. This resolution, however, prohibited abortion funding except when the life of the mother is endangered or pregnancy results from rape or incest. This is stricter language than the 1978 amendment, which provided funding for abortions when the life of the mother is endangered, when pregnancy results from rape or incest, or when severe and long-lasting physical health damage is certified.[20]

In fact, 1979 was not a very good year for the pro-choice forces in Congress in part because of the electoral defeats of such strong pro-choice advocates as Senator Edward Brooke (R–Mass.). The right-to-life strategy of chipping away everywhere seemed to gain new adherents. Whereas the FY 1979 Department of Defense appropriations bill allowed some funding for abortions, the FY 1980 Defense appropriations bill was more restrictive, with abortion funding for Department of Defense personnel limited to life endangerment, rape, or incest. For the Foreign Assistance appropriations bill, the Senate as well as the House agreed to prohibit any money to be used for abortions for Peace Corps volunteers even in cases

[19] *NARAL Newsletter* 11 (Sept. 1979), 5.
[20] *NARAL Newsletter* 12 (Jan. 1980), 6.

of life endangerment. And in 1979 the FY 1980 District of Columbia appropriations bill became the target of anti-choice forces. Representative Robert Dornan (R–Calif.) introduced an amendment that would have prohibited the use of all D.C. funds, including those raised by local tax sources, to pay for abortions except in cases of life endangerment. However, the Senate D.C. Appropriations Committee Chairman, Senator Patrick Leahy (D–Vt.), and the ranking minority member, Senator Charles Mathias, Jr. (R–Md.), have records supporting abortions under the Medicaid program and thus backed modifications in the Dornan amendment. They facilitated a loosening of the anti-choice language in response to both D.C. home rule pressure and pro-choice forces.[21] Whereas the House of Representatives supported the Dornan amendment by a vote of 217-210,[22] the Senate, led by Senator Leahy, defeated the same amendment, offered in the Senate by Senator Jesse Helms (R–N.C.), by a vote of 55-34.[23] As the D.C. appropriations bill was enacted, federal funds to the District of Columbia could fund abortions only in cases of life endangerment, rape, or incest. However, any and all abortions could be funded with locally raised money.[24] Also, and of potentially more serious consequence to pro-choice forces, the House of Representatives on December 6, 1979, supported by a vote of 217-169 an amendment introduced by Representative Harold Volkmer (D–Mo.) to the Child Health Assurance Program (CHAP) that would prohibit Medicaid funding for abortions except when necessary to save the life of the mother.[25] Such an amendment would change Title XIX of the Social Security Act, which is the Medicaid statute. This would have a more lasting impact than the yearly amendments to the appropriations bill to restrict Medicaid-funded abortions since an amendment to CHAP would be included in the authorization

---

[21] *Washington Post*, July 19, 1979, B1 and B17.
[22] *Washington Post*, Sept. 24, 1979, C1.
[23] *NARAL Newsletter* 11 (Sept. 1979), 5 and 8.
[24] *Ibid.* and *NARAL Newsletter* 12 (Jan. 1980), 6.
[25] *NARAL Newsletter* 12 (Feb. 1980), 11.

language and authorizations, unlike appropriations, are not subject to yearly review and approval. Moreover, this amendment, if enacted, would interfere with court orders to fund abortions because the court orders are based in part on what is included in the Medicaid statute.[26]

Women's groups and the coalition lobbying to protect choice had learned to be satisfied with "fuzzy" language as a compromise between some choice and no choice at all. In 1979 they were clearly unsuccessful in maintaining even loose anti-choice language. Their congressional lobbying efforts failed, especially in the Senate where the language of the original Hyde amendment was the language approved and sent to conference committee.

At the state level, all legislatures have felt the continuing pressure of anti-abortion lobbyists, since the Hyde amendment deprives states of matching federal funds for Medicaid abortions except under Hyde criteria and thus leaves it up to states whether or not to continue funding on their own. As a result, state after state has curtailed public funding of abortion, eliminating the access of lower-income women to legal abortion. By 1980 fifteen states had supported a constitutional amendment limiting abortion rights.

It should be noted that a *Congressional Quarterly (CQ)* analysis of 25 roll calls on the abortion issue found that lobbying had little impact; 415 representatives never wavered on their position. What the study did find was that religion was the key predictor of voting, with two-thirds of Catholic representatives taking a staunchly anti-abortion position, though some Catholics, such as Father Drinan (then Democratic Representative from Massachusetts), have been in the forefront of congressional pro-choice forces. Senate Catholics were less numerous and more divided on abortion. Blacks generally

---

[26] *NARAL Newsletter* 12 (Jan. 1980), 6. Other congressional restrictions include a prohibition on consideration of abortion issues by the U.S. Commission on Civil Rights, exclusion of abortion cases from coverage by federally funded legal services, and the anti-abortion (Beard) amendment of the Pregnancy Disability Act.

opposed limits on abortion, as did 12 of the 18 women in Congress, thus fragmenting the Congressional Women's Caucus on this issue. Although voting on abortion-related issues crosses partisan lines, the CQ analysis reveals a degree of issue congruence apparent in voting on abortion. A substantial majority of abortion opponents voted against welfare measures, too, suggesting that while this is not strictly a liberal/conservative issue, elements of ideology play a considerable role.[27] Despite CQ's finding that lobbying per se does not necessarily influence individual congressional voting on abortion, many members of Congress perceive the existence of a highly mobilized, single-issue-focused anti-abortion constituency and vote accordingly. As John Kingdon has shown, when constituency positions are perceived as intense, as on racial matters, and are viewed as having high salience, a member of Congress will vote with his or her constituents.[28] Kingdon also adds that interest-group activity is likely to be of concern in congressional decision making insofar as it is connected with a strong constituency base and accords with preexisting values.[29] A recent article has contended that "the abortion issue has produced the most highly charged lobbying since the contentious days of the Vietnam war."[30]

Anti-abortion views are internalized for many members of Congress through deeply held religious and ideological values. Hence overt lobbying tactics may not always be necessary. In addition, pro-life groups have "hit lists" of people in Congress to defeat and, through effective focusing of resources, may have had an intimidating effect on voting in this matter. The widely publicized defeat of pro-choice Senator Dick Clark of Iowa in 1978, mobilized through massive telephone surveys, pro-life mailings, and leaflets distributed to thousands of state

[27] *CQ Weekly Report*, Feb. 4, 1978, 258-60.

[28] John Kingdon, *Congressmen's Voting Decisions* (New York: Harper and Row, 1973), 41.

[29] *Ibid.*, 57-60.

[30] *New York Times*, June 26, 1977, Sect. IV, 10.

residents may have served notice on numerous other members of Congress to "vote right"—against funding for abortions.

The Pro-Life Action Committee, which singled out Clark as a target, distributed 300,000 pamphlets through churches at a total cost of less than $10,000. Senator Clark's pro-life opponent won by 26,000 votes; a *Des Moines Register* election-day survey found that 25,000 people voted against Clark because of his position on abortion, thereby *almost* providing the margin of defeat.[31] The defeat of Representative Donald Fraser in Minnesota in 1978 also turned in part on the right-to-life issue, as well as on questions of continued welfare-state liberalism with which abortion is often associated (as did Senator Clark's Iowa race).

The 1980 Senate elections saw a concerted effort by abortion opponents to defeat pro-choice candidates. Their widely publicized efforts were successful in aiding in the defeat of Birch Bayh (D–Ind.), George McGovern (D–S.D.), Frank Church (D–Idaho), and other liberals. The right-wing National Conservative Political Action Committee (NCPAC), working in conjunction with the Life Amendment Political Action Committee (LAPAC) and the Moral Majority, poured millions of dollars (an estimated 5 million) into the campaign against incumbents they had targeted for defeat. In contrast, NARAL could raise only $250,000 for candidates it supported.[32] As a result, in the 98th Congress the Senate Appropriations, Budget, Finance, and Judiciary Committees all have anti-abortion rather than pro-choice leadership.

There is a well-developed network of conservative activists—including Catholic and some fundamentalist and Mormon church groups as well as several traditional right-wing organizations—that have focused on the abortion issue and have sought to persuade members of Congress that voters are single-issue oriented and that a pro-choice vote would spell

[31] *New York Times*, Nov. 13, 1978, 18.

[32] *NARAL Newsletter* 12 (Dec. 1980), 1, 4-5. See also *New York Times*, Nov. 7, 1980, A16, and Richard Cohen, "Congressional Focus," *National Journal*, Nov. 18, 1980, 1960.

certain electoral defeat. This belief is widely held despite the fact that the feminist groups contend that, of the nineteen Representatives who lost their seats in 1976, only four had voted pro-choice.[33]

THE GROUP ACTORS

Pro-Lifers

In the wake of the Supreme Court decision in *Roe* v. *Wade* and the congressional debates on the Hyde and other anti-choice amendments, an angry and highly organized group of women (and men) have mobilized against abortion rights. At the state conventions in 1977 held under the auspices of the International Women's Year as well as in other public forums, such as the 1980 White House Conference on the Family, opposition to state ratification of the ERA and to abortion on demand surfaced and demonstrated conflict among women at the grassroots level regarding abortion policy (although at the White House conferences, pro-choice groups generally prevailed). Ellen McCormack ran for President in 1976 on a right-to-life platform, and in 1978 in New York State the Right-to-Life Party gained sufficient voters to qualify automatically for inclusion on the ballot in future years.

In January 1980 some fifty leaders of right-to-life groups met in Washington for three days to plan their strategies of political activism and to prepare for their "March for Life" on the Capitol, held yearly on the anniversary of the Supreme Court's decision in *Roe* v. *Wade*. The conference was co-sponsored by the Life Amendment Political Action Committee and Christian Family Renewal. One particularly interesting point was made at this meeting by Paul Weyrich, Director of the Committee for the Survival of a Free Congress, a conservative political action group. He noted: "It doesn't matter what the majority of the American people think on a poll.

[33] Interview with Linda Lipson, Congressional Clearinghouse for Women's Rights, Sept. 1, 1977.

What matters is the perception members of Congress have about your issue and their future."[34] Pro-choice forces have had difficulty in dealing with this problem. In part they have because pro-choice groups are often unable to compete with the right-to-life groups that are organized around a single issue and that employ tactics appealing to fear and emotion. The belief that an intense minority may prevail even against popular opinion thus gains credence. Consider for a moment the statement of Carolyn Thompson, Chairperson of the Pro-Life Action Committee, the political arm of Iowa's anti-abortion movement. In discussing the 1980 Iowa caucuses to elect delegates to the national convention, she noted: "Most people are going to sit by the fire that night and not bother to go out. That's why a special interest group like ourselves can be so effective, because if we make any effort at all to turn our people out, we can take the delegation."[35]

In addition, the right-to-life groups are deeply involved in the use of the language of morality and religion and present themselves as the defenders of moral righteousness acting against the pro-choice groups that, in contradistinction, are represented as the forces of anti-morality, anti-religion, and anti-God. Robert Moffett, administrative assistant to Representative Robert Dornan (R–Calif.), suggested that the anti-choice movement, by identifying itself as the "Right-to-Life Movement," has absorbed the moral tenets of Judeo-Christain faith. Further, he noted that if anti-choice is identified as "right-to-life," pro-choice becomes identified to many people as "anti-life." He drew some parallels between the contemporary pro-life movement and the anti-war movement in the late 1960s and early 1970s. The anti-war movement was identified as morally good and supportive of life and thus, by extension, if you were not against war, you were identified as for war and therefore for killing, death, and destruction.[36]

The National Right to Life Committee, an umbrella organ-

[34] *New York Times*, Jan. 21, 1980, 22.
[35] *New York Times*, Jan. 12, 1980, 22.
[36] Interview with Robert Moffett, U.S. Congress, Oct. 10, 1979.

ization, is the largest on either side of the abortion controversy; claiming 11 million active supporters in 3,000 chapters,
with formidable grassroots strength and a $3 million annual
budget. The Catholic Church has been a major institutional
and financial force behind right-to-life activities, although
Mormons, Orthodox Jews, and Protestant fundamentalists
have also been active.

The right-to-life position of the Catholic Church is rooted
initially in the 1869 prohibition of all abortions by Pope Pius
IX. The 1968 papal encyclical *Humanae Vitae* reaffirmed
Church opposition to abortion. In 1975 the Catholic Bishops
of the United States approved unanimously a "Pastoral Plan
for Pro-Life Activities." This Pastoral Plan "seeks to activate
the pastoral resources of the Church in three major efforts:
(1) educational . . . ; (2) a pastoral effort . . .; (3) a public
policy effort directed toward the legislative, judicial and administrative areas so as to insure effective legal protection for
the right to life."[37]

An interview with Rev. Bryce, head of the Committee for
Pro-Life Activities of the National Conference of Catholic
Bishops, revealed that abortion is seen as an issue that serves
to mobilize Church activists and is therefore an issue of unusual—and more than strictly spiritual—importance for the
Church hierarchy. The Church's political activities are, of course,
tax exempt.[38]

It should be noted that despite the organized effort of the
Catholic Church to ban all abortions, Catholics as a group
are not opposed to abortion; differences between Catholics
and Protestants on this issue are relatively slight and continue
to narrow.[39] A 1977 CBS News and *New York Times* poll
asking "Should the right of a woman to have an abortion be
left entirely to the woman and her doctor?" was repeated in
1979 (see Table 9). To a second query, asking whether the

[37] "Pastoral Plan for Pro-Life Activities," *The Wanderer* 108 (Dec. 14,
1975).

[38] Interview with Rev. Edward M. Bryce, Sept. 18, 1978.

[39] Skerry, "The Class Conflict over Abortion," 74.

government should help a poor woman with her abortion bills, 47 percent of Protestant respondents and 43 percent of Catholic respondents answered "yes." A 1977 Gallup Poll found 53 percent of Catholic respondents agreeing with 58 percent of Protestant respondents that abortion should be legal "under some circumstances."[40]

Despite this apparent split in Catholic opinion, Church support of the right-to-life position remains unyielding. As the executive director of the National Right to Life Committee put it: "The only reason we have a movement in this nation is because of the Catholic people and the Catholic Church. The rest of us would hardly make a ripple." It is possible that Catholic domination of the movement should be seen as a consequence of the sheer organizational power of the Church—the most centralized church bureaucracy in the United States, catering to the single largest denomination.[41]

In addition to the right-to-life activities of the National Conference of Catholic Bishops, there are groups of lay Catholics such as the National Committee for a Human Life Amendment. William Cox, director of this committee, claims that his group is separate from the National Conference of Catholic Bishops but does receive money from dioceses and the National Conference. The primary goal of Cox's group

TABLE 9

Should the Right to Have an Abortion Be Left
Entirely to the Woman and Her Doctor?

	Disagree		Agree		No Opinion	
	1977	1979	1977	1979	1977	1979
Protestants	21%	27%	76%	69%	3%	4%
Catholics	26%	32%	68%	64%	5%	4%

SOURCE: *New York Times*, Nov. 11, 1979.

[40] NARAL, "Polls on Abortion," Jan, 1978; and *New York Times*, Nov. 11, 1979, 43.

[41] Skerry, "The Class Conflict over Abortion," 74.

and other anti-choice groups is to secure an anti-abortion amendment to the Constitution.[42] The secondary goal of this group is to secure right-to-life legislative amendments such as the Hyde amendment. These two goals are shared by virtually all right-to-life groups. There is some overlap between this lay Catholic organization and other right-to-life groups such as the National Right to Life Committee, which is nonsectarian, American Citizens Concerned for Life, and the Catholic League for Religious and Civil Rights.[43] They are organized into a loose coalition known as the "Life Lobby."

Some of the techniques utilized by "Right to Lifers" have already been indicated above. The 1975 Bishops' Pastoral Plan calls for a sophisticated network of parish committees to carry out anti-abortion work. These are organized along congressional district lines to facilitate mobilization of political action groups each with an assigned pro-life political coordinator.[44] Activists have been organized to work in electoral and party politics and to lobby at the state and national level. Money is raised on such occasions as "Respect Life" Sunday and through Catholic Charities. William Cox likened the techniques used by the Church in what is probably its most sophisticated political effort to date to those employed by Common Cause and the anti-war movement.[45]

In addition to traditional political techniques, right-to-life activists have also organized demonstrations including the annual March for Life to protest the anniversary of the 1973 Supreme Court decision. The January 1979 March attracted 60,000 people to Washington.[46] In recent years some right-to-life forces have expanded their activities from the legislative

[42] Interview with William Cox, Director, National Right to Life Committee, Sept. 29, 1978.

[43] *Ibid.*

[44] *Women Under Attack: Abortion, Sterilization Abuse and Reproductive Freedom* (New York: Committee for Abortion Rights and Against Sterilization Abuse, 1979), 32.

[45] Interview with William Cox.

[46] *New York Times*, Jan. 23, 1979, C10.

and electoral arenas to conduct a campaign of harassment and violence against abortion clinics. For example, Joseph Scheidler, director of a Chicago group called Friends for Life, has criticized a public view, prompted by fire bombings of abortion clinics in several states, that "pro-life is violent." However, though he does not personally advocate violence to achieve anti-abortion goals, he has noted that "I don't cry real hard when I hear about one of their fire traps burning down."[47]

The conflict over abortion pits women against one another. The Ad Hoc Committee in Defense of Life, an anti-abortion group that publishes a biweekly newsletter, *Life-letter*, counts numerous women as members, as do other similar groups. A study of anti-ERA activists, who often have overlapping memberships in right-to-life groups, has found that these women are formidable adversaries for the women's rights groups. They often are middle to upper class in background, educated, motivated to activism by traditional social values and religious beliefs, and they are active political participants with a strong sense of efficacy.[48]

An interview with Anne O'Donnell, director of the National Right to Life Committee, revealed a somewhat different perspective. In her view abortion politics involves a "class struggle" owing to the predominantly lower- and middle-class character of right-to-life activists, who are also engaged in intensive religious activity.[49] Again, despite their reputation as single-issue groups, Right to Lifers have alliances and linkages to anti-ERA and conservative, anti-government, anti-gun control, and other right-wing forces. Increasingly, some students of abortion politics have come to view pro-life activists as those who would "reprivatize" a whole set of policy issues,

[47] *Ibid.*

[48] David Brody and Kent Tedin, "Ladies in Pink: Religion and Political Ideology in the Anti-ERA Movement," *Social Science Quarterly* 56 (March 1976), 72–82.

[49] Interview with Anne O'Donnell, Director, National Right to Life Committee, Sept. 28, 1979. See also Skerry, "The Class Conflict over Abortion," who suggests the relevance of the class conflict model as well.

including Medicaid, health care, and abortion. Such reprivatization of social welfare functions would have as its ultimate goal the dismantling of the entire welfare state.[50]

The Feminist Response

Women's groups including the Women's Lobby, NWPC AAUW, and NOW began to work together in June 1977 as part of a pro-choice coalition along with NARAL, Planned Parenthood, and the ACLU belatedly to influence the legislative process. A coalition of twenty-seven women's groups did, for example, urge President Carter to reconsider his opposition to Federal funding for abortions—with no tangible results. In addition, a group of twenty organizations have joined together into the Abortion Information Exchange, and for several years they have met biweekly to plan strategy. Their efforts are buttressed by local groups such as CARASA (Committee for Abortion Rights and Against Sterilization Abuse), oriented toward community-based efforts to gain and expand reproductive freedom. But, unlike the "other side," many feminist groups have been forced to devote their limited resources and leadership to other issues as well.[51]

Third-party support has been notably absent. Neither the NAACP, the Leadership Conference on Civil Rights, labor unions, Common Cause, nor the powerful medical community have been willing to be extensively involved in this controversial issue—though the American Medical Association has endorsed the pro-choice view on abortion. Analysis of the politics of reproductive freedom by social historians suggests that physicians and other health professionals have traditionally been reluctant to cede control over reproductive self-de-

[50] Rosalind Petchesky, "The Courts, the State and the Medical Model of Abortion: Rethinking the Feminist View Since Harris v. McRae" (paper presented at the Northeast Political Science Association convention, New Haven, Conn., Nov. 21, 1980), 50-53.

[51] *New York Times*, Aug. 3, 1977, 9.

termination solely to women.[52] Traditional groups such as the League of Women Voters have sought to remain aloof from the abortion issue. Among civil rights allies, support has been forthcoming on the abortion issue from Jesse Jackson's "Operation Push" and the Congressional Black Caucus, which under the aegis of Congressman Louis Stokes (D–Ohio) issued a pro-choice letter.

Organizations such as NARAL, which is probably the most active group in the pro-choice movement, have grown dramatically in recent years as they have sought to counter the grassroots efforts of the Right to Lifers. NARAL has grown from 20,000 to 90,000 members; a self-survey reveals a membership that is white, female, urban, disproportionately Jewish, and relatively young (25-44). A large number of members come from the Middle Atlantic states, and many are professionally educated and professionally employed. Members consider themselves liberals, and there is a substantial overlap between NARAL membership and that of other feminist groups including NOW and pro-choice groups such as the ACLU and Planned Parenthood.[53] The NARAL survey lends credence to the view the pro-choice activists represent a far different women's constituency than the Right to Lifers.

NARAL derives virtually all of its resources from its membership; these now total over one and a half million dollars annually. A tax-exempt (501) (c) (3) foundation funded in part by Stewart Mott aids in public relations and media-related activities. NARAL itself, however, does not have tax-exempt status; it must derive virtually all of its funds from membership dues and contributions. Also, although by the end of the 1970s NARAL began to organize state and local

[52] See Hayler, "Abortion," 312, and Linda Gordon, *Women's Body, Women's Right* (New York: Grossman, 1976). Hayler quotes studies suggesting physicians' negative attitudes toward abortion, unless performed for strictly medical reasons (315).

[53] Robert Cameron Mitchell, John D. McCarthy, and Kathy Pearch, *Report on a Membership Survey* (Washington, D.C.: NARAL, April 9, 1979).

affiliates more diligently, the right-to-life movement had started much earlier and had a substantial headstart on grassroots organizations via the Church. Nonetheless, NARAL and other groups have recognized the importance of moving beyond the national legislative arena and building local organizations. Such efforts appear essential, as a *New York Times* thirteen-state survey revealed that "in nearly every state, abortion rights advocates have failed to equal the opponent's network of dedicated and steady if often modest contributors or, more often than not, cannot turn out equivalent busloads of demonstrators."[54] In addition to NARAL's local efforts, the Religious Coalition for Abortion Rights (RCAR) and the ACLU-RFP have hired field coordinators, are recruiting state and local coordinators, and are reordering priorities and resources.[55] Groups such as Planned Parenthood, interested in family planning in general, have a substantial community affiliate base (183 affiliates in 43 states) and have become increasingly active in pro-choice, reproductive freedom issues.

Feminists have made other attempts to remain vigilant and counter the backlash against reproductive rights. Among these has been electoral politics. The NARAL Political Action Committee claimed that, of nineteen candidates to whose campaigns it contributed in 1978, 71 percent were elected. NARAL also successfully fought an anti-abortion ballot in Oregon in that year.[56] In 1980 NARAL adopted the strategy of electoral "hit lists" used successfully by the other side and organized a Political Action Committee (Impact 80) to support pro-choice candidates for public office, including Presidential candidate John Anderson.

A group called Voters for Choice, financed by contributions, was organized to "target" anti-abortion members of Congress in 1980 as well. Despite the general inability of pro-choice groups to positively affect election results, NARAL claimed

[54] *New York Times*, Oct. 23, 1977, 24.

[55] Jeanne Bell Nicholson and Debra Stewart, "The Supreme Court, Abortion Policy and State Response," *Publius* 8 (Winter 1978), 176.

[56] Letter from Karen Mulhauser, Executive Director, NARAL.

victory in two primary races in Massachusetts, with the election of two pro-choice candidates for Congress (notwithstanding a widely circulated letter from the local Cardinal opposing them). A pro-choice candidate was also chosen to succeed Representative John Anderson in Illinois.

And, though unsuccessful in influencing the outcomes of the 1980 Presidential race and several key senatorial races, feminist delegates to the Democratic national convention were able to gain platform support for a pro-choice plank including federal abortion funding (as well as for support of the ERA) by utilizing their numerical strength and group cohesion to advantage. The Republican platform took an opposing view on abortion and the ERA, even advocating selection of pro-life federal judges, thus providing voters with a clear-cut issue choice. (The results of the 1980 vote, which did demonstrate a women's vote distinct from that of men, will be considered in Chapter 8).

Feminists have also sought to litigate abortion-related issues. The ACLU announced abortion as a priority concern in 1978. Its RFP joined with Planned Parenthood and the Center for Constitutional Rights (all groups active in litigating on behalf of reproductive freedom) to bring *Harris* v. *McRae*,[57] a class-action suit, into Federal Court, representing the interests of lower-class women who had been denied Medicaid abortions. The suit alleged a violation of separation of church and state and infringement of the rights of privacy, due process, and equal protection.

On January 15, 1980, some thirty-nine months after the *McRae* case was introduced, Judge John F. Dooling, Jr., of the Federal District Court of Brooklyn, New York, ordered government officials to resume authorizing the expenditure of federal Medicaid funds to help pay for "medically necessary abortions provided by duly certified providers." Judge Dooling held that not to provide such services was "to violate the pregnant woman's First and Fifth Amendment rights." He

[57] 429 U.S. 129.

further held that a decision to have a medically necessary abortion was an exercise of a woman's "most fundamental of rights, nearly allied to her right to be, surely part of the liberty protected by the Fifth Amendment, doubly protected when the liberty is exercised in conformity with the religious belief and teaching protected by the First Amendment."[58]

However, on June 30, 1980, the Supreme Court (by a vote of 5-4) refused to reinstate the obligation of states to finance abortions for poor women. The Court upheld the Hyde amendment's curtailment of federal funding at any stage of pregnancy, for any reason other than to save a woman's life. The decision concluded that "abortion is inherently different from other medical procedures, because no other procedure involves the purposeful termination of a potential life." This marks a retreat from the *Roe* v. *Wade* position, which seemed to suggest a woman's fundamental right to abortion, at least until the third trimester.[59] Other judicial efforts by women's rights groups have been able to limit further the erosion of "free choice" by preventing parents or husbands from vetoing the right to have an abortion (*Bellotti* v. *Baird*[60] and *Planned Parenthood of Central Missouri* v. *Danforth*[61])—though in *H——L——* v. *Matheson*[62] the Court upheld parental consent for abortions performed on minors.

Rights groups have been divided regarding strategies on how to proceed. The question has been raised as to whether it would be more effective to counter the pro-life advocates and their emotional appeals with demonstrations showing photos of women who have died as a result of self-induced abortions or to work through the traditional political process. Right-to-life groups are willing to make any appeals to aid their cause. In general, as is true for the feminist movement

[58] *New York Times*, Jan. 16, 1980, A1 and B2.

[59] See Petchesky, "The Courts, the State and the Medical Model of Abortion."

[60] 428 U.S. 132 (1976).

[61] 1428 U.S. 52 (1976).

[62] L.W. No. 79-5903 (1981).

as a whole, pro-choice groups have adhered to traditional political techniques (at least since the early 1970s) and have not resorted to protest or "guerilla theatre." Pro-choice advocates in a rare demonstration did deliver 200 coat hangers to Representative Daniel Flood (D–Pa.), then chair of the Labor and Health, Education, and Welfare Subcommittee of the House Appropriations Committee, as a reminder of old methods of abortion.[63] Still, even the name "pro-choice" is designed to present a moderate, nonthreatening tone to this branch of the feminist movement.

In the pro-choice community NARAL is the major single-issue membership group that has abortion rights as its sole focus. Other groups such as Planned Parenthood, the ACLU, and NOW serve other constituencies as well and differ in singularity of purpose. Only the Religious Coalition for Abortion Rights shares NARAL's exclusive interest in the abortion issue. The coalescence of pro-choice groups with feminist groups provides additional strength; at the same time money and activism, already in short supply, are diffused into numerous policy areas. However, the existence of a separate pro-choice coalition has freed the larger feminist movement from continual focus on this issue and has also served to separate the controversial abortion issue from other feminist goals in the minds of policy makers. This has had the effect of preventing defeats on abortion from causing a general anti-feminist spillover—different feminist issues appear to be separable in the congressional political psyche.

The vast majority of the American public certainly seems to support "free choice." A 1980 poll by the New York City firm of Dresner and Tortorello commissioned by NARAL found that 88 percent of registered voters believe in the right to choose abortion depending upon circumstances that relate to a woman's life, health, or victimization by rape or incest.[64] These results are not at variance with other survey findings.

[63] *New York Times*, Sept. 8, 1979, Sect. III, 11.
[64] *NARAL Newsletter* 12 (Feb. 1980), 1.

Thus the June 1979 issue of *Redbook* magazine carried the results of a poll it commissioned from the Gallup organization in which 80 percent of Americans are shown to believe that abortion should be legal at least under some circumstances.[65] It should be noted, however, that support for "free choice" varies with the circumstances involved and with the period in which the abortion is sought. In addition, a small majority of the population appears to oppose federal funding for abortions, perhaps motivated as much by opposition to welfare spending as to abortion.[66] Hence the abortion issue is one in which significant counterpressures have been generated in a political climate hostile to continuing or even sustaining abortion reform but in which the vast majority of people support some aspects of "free choice."

CONCLUSION

At the outset of this analysis it was hypothesized that feminists have been most successful in the political process when they are able to "contain" a political issue, stress its technical aspects over which they may present a monopoly of information, and limit the degree to which debate becomes public. Abortion fits none of these criteria. In addition, it was postulated that the broader the issue and the more threatening to prevailing values—the more it represents role change as opposed to role equity—the more difficult will be efforts to contain conflict and prevent countermobilization.

We have suggested that the issue of abortion choice appears to threaten traditional family values and lifestyles; it is an issue that portends fundamental change in women's role in society, for reproductive freedom provides an alternative to compulsory motherhood and family life. Thus it is the most difficult type of issue on which to gain change. The feminist movement has sought to counter the immense power of the

[65] Reported in *NARAL Newsletter* 11 (May-June 1979), 16.
[66] *New York Times*, July 29, 1977, 1, and April 21, 1979, 49.

Catholic Church in partnership with the right-to-life movement that it supports monetarily and spiritually. Feminists have endeavored to reorder their priorities and focus, though limited by lack of resources and personnel. Through continued legislative lobbying, bringing court suits, building grassroots strength, and engaging in electoral and campaign activity, feminists are seeking to regain the ground they have lost. It is likely that they will succeed in preventing an anti-abortion constitutional amendment, owing to the difficulties associated with the amendment process. Nonetheless, abortion remains an issue that tears the women's constituency apart with conflict, that has stirred deep-seated moral and religious values, and that remains highly controversial.

CHAPTER 7

THE PREGNANCY DISABILITY ACT AND COALITION POLITICS

INTRODUCTION

The campaign to reverse the Supreme Court's 1976 decision in *General Electric* v. *Gilbert*[1] and to amend Title VII of the Civil Rights Act of 1964 to prohibit sex discrimination on the basis of pregnancy seemed at the outset to reveal political patterns similar to those which existed for equal credit opportunity. Pregnancy disability is a relatively narrow role equity issue that involves no public outlay of funds and that deals with matters of potential benefit to all women. However, since the issue deals with pregnant women and therefore the potential role of women as mothers and homemakers, it was fraught with more controversy than the Equal Credit Opportunity Act had been, especially since the question of funding abortions under disability plans received particular attention from opponents of "free choice."

Unlike the credit issue, the Pregnancy Disability Act, which at the outset of the congressional deliberations seemed likely to gain speedy approval with only limited opposition, foundered under attacks from anti-abortion forces. However, the time elapsed from the moment the Supreme Court handed down its decision to the final passage of the law was just under two years. The act, as finally passed, does contain the anti-abortion amendment introduced by Representative Edward Beard (D–

[1] 429 U.S. 125.

154

R.I.). Nonetheless, the successful effort to overturn the Supreme Court's *Gilbert* decision marked a coalitional response by an unusually broad-based cross section of groups including feminist and other women's organizations, labor and civil rights forces, and some right-to-life groups as well.

The issue of pregnancy disability has taken on a role of increased significance for the feminist movement as labor force participation by women has grown. Pregnancy has been used as a rationale for providing different and inequitable treatment for women in the work force, and thus the relatively narrow issue of pregnancy-disability insurance has ramifications of both a symbolic and practical nature—particularly in an era when five times as many mothers are working as in 1950, and when more than 60 percent of women in the 25-54 age range are in the work force, triple the percentage in the years immediately following World War II.[2]

BACKGROUND

Prior to World War II and the domestic manpower shortage that accompanied the national military mobilization, it was assumed that women, when they worked outside of the home, did so only until marriage or childrearing responsibilities removed them from the work force. In other words, women belonged in the home. There were several consequences for the labor force that emerged in the 1920s and 1930s as a result of this belief.[3] Often women were barred from employment or dismissed when they became married. A 1930-31 National Education Association (NEA) study indicated that 77 percent of surveyed districts would not hire wives and 63 percent dismissed female teachers if they married. During

---

[2] Peg Simpson, "A Victory for Women," *Civil Rights Digest* 11 (Spring 1979), 17.

[3] This discussion relies heavily upon the testimony of Wendy M. Williams before U.S. Senate, Committee on Labor and Human Resources, Labor Subcommittee, *Discrimination on the Basis of Pregnancy, 1977* (Washington, D.C.: U.S. Government Printing Office, 1977), 122-47.

the 1920s there was a movement to provide workers with fringe benefits. The idea behind the fringe-benefit movement was that a company could attract and then hold good workers by generating security and loyalty. Thus fringe benefits that would benefit the employee would ultimately benefit the employer as well. Inasmuch as women were identified as being marginal workers whose primary roles were those of wives and mothers, limitations were imposed on the benefits made available to them. Some companies just allowed women fewer benefits, but other companies excluded women totally from being eligible for benefits.

As noted previously, during World War II many women—4.5 million—entered the work force. Although there was a need to reassess employment policies and practices, and both the War Manpower Commission and the Children's Bureau issued studies recommending change, women's jobs were terminated once the war effort ended without regard to seniority or employment aspirations, and for the most part pre-war patterns of discrimination in employment reemerged. The author of the Children's Bureau study contended that although protection of mother and fetus as well as fear of liability for miscarriage was the justification given for termination of a pregnant women from employment, often there were aesthetic and moral reasons at the root of these practices—it was "not nice" for pregnant women to work and it had a "bad effect" on male workers.

In 1964, when Title VII of the Civil Rights Act was enacted, conditions for women in the work force were such that 40 percent of all employers did not even provide unpaid maternity leave—pregnant women were just fired. Among those employers who did provide maternity leave, over 50 percent required women to go on leave before their seventh month of pregnancy. Only 6 percent permitted female workers to use sick leave for pregnancy-related illness or disability.

Title VII's impact upon employment discrimination against women was considerable, and regarding pregnancy in particular, it was dramatic: 73 percent of female workers by 1973 were entitled to maternity leave and reemployment rights; 26 percent could use sick leave for pregnancy-related disability of illness.

When the Supreme Court, in *General Electric* v. *Gilbert*, decided that denial of benefits for pregnancy-related disability and illness is not discrimination based on sex, several questions regarding employment opportunities for women emerged onto center stage. It is estimated that approximately 80 percent of all women become pregnant at some point in their working lives. Even women who do not become pregnant are viewed as potentially pregnant by their employers until they pass childbearing age. As Wendy Williams observed in her testimony at hearings before the Labor Subcommittee of U.S. Senate Committee on Labor and Human Resources: "Thus, all women are subject to the effects of the stereotype that women are marginal workers with the multifaceted consequences this has for hiring, job assignment, promotion, pay, and fringe benfits."[4] When women have been forced to take unpaid leave, they have often lost their benefits—including accrued retirement benefits, vacation leave, and sick leave—as well as their seniority. Thus, if promotion opportunities are to be based upon time spent in a position, women who have lost their seniority owing to unpaid leaves often have been locked into low-paying positions.

The entire question of rights for working women had become crucial to labor market considerations by the time the Supreme Court issued its decision in the *Gilbert* case. Whereas in 1950 women comprised 29.6 percent of the labor force and 33.8 percent of all women were employed, by 1977 women comprised 41 percent of the labor force and nearly one-half of all women were working outside of their homes.[5] Also, women were clustered in low-paid, low-status positions. If pregnancy-disability benefits were to be denied women, their

[4] *Ibid.*, 130-31.

[5] U.S. Department of Labor, Bureau of Labor Statistics, *Handbook of Labor Statistics, 1978* (Washington, D.C.: U.S. Government Printing Office, 1978).

status would have been further worsened at a time when more and more women found it necessary to work, because they were either supporting their families as heads of households or helping keep their families, with another employed member, out of conditions of poverty.

THE CAMPAIGN TO OVERTURN THE GILBERT DECISION

The effort to define pregnancy as a disability for insurance purposes is similar in some ways to the anti-abortion Hyde amendment, in that it has involved a legislative attempt to overturn a Supreme Court decision, albeit from the opposite side of the political spectrum.

The Equal Employment Opportunities Commission (EEOC) was established by the Civil Rights Act of 1964 to implement Title VII prohibiting discrimination by employers on the basis of sex. But the role of the EEOC has been a limited one to date.[6] Not until 1972 did the EEOC issue guidelines requiring that pregnancy and related conditions be treated as disabilities for employment purposes. And, even then, the EEOC was known to be understaffed, weak, inefficient, and deluged with complaints. Hence feminists and other relevant interest groups turned to the federal courts for enforcement of rights. (The EEOC did participate in *Gilbert* and other related cases as *amicus* because of its concern with the validity of pregnancy guidelines.)

In December 1976 the Supreme Court held in *General Electric* v. *Gilbert* that refusal to extend disability benefits to pregnant women is not discrimination based on sex. The Court's decision was not entirely unexpected, following as it did the 1974 decision in *Gedulig* v. *Aiello*,[7] which upheld California's

[6] Carol Greenwald, "Women's Rights, Courts and Congress: Conflict Over Pregnancy Disability Compensation Policies" (paper presented at the American Political Science Association convention, Sept. 3, 1978), 24-25.

[7] 417 U.S. 484.

refusal to pay pregnancy disability benefits to female workers.[8] The Supreme Court's majority opinion in *Gilbert*, written by Justice Rehnquist, found that the exclusion of pregnancy and pregnancy-related disabilities from coverage under an otherwise comprehensive temporary disabilities plan was not a violation of Title VII's prohibition of discrimination "against any individual with respect to his compensation, terms, conditions or privileges of employment because of . . . race, color, religion, sex or national origin."[9] According to Rehnquist, General Electric's policy was "facially neutral"; since the nature of exemption was pregnancy and not pregnant women, there was no sex discrimination.

The *Gilbert* case arose from a suit brought by the International Union of Electrical, Radio, and Machine Workers (IUE) and argued by its attorney, Ruth Weyand, although *amicus* briefs were submitted by several feminist groups including the Women Rights Project (ACLU), WLDF, and WEAL. Weyand's filing of a lengthy set of briefs, totalling 250 pages, apparently incurred the wrath of the jurists, perhaps limiting the impact of the case presented by feminists.[10]

The Court's decision in the *Gilbert* case engendered the development of a coalition of groups in support of women's interests in pregnancy disability. In this instance, a widespread network was activated within days of the adverse Court decision of December 1976, and a coalition with over three hundred groups participating was developed. Labor union backing was especially strong on this issue. Church groups and even some Right to Lifers were among the original members of this broad-based coalition, known as the Campaign

---

[8] The Court's record with regard to maternity and pregnancy cases has been, to say the least, prone to inconsistency. In another 1974 case, *Cleveland Board of Education* v. *La Fleur* (414 U.S. 663), a law requiring teachers to leave their positions when five months pregnant was declared unconstitutional.

[9] *General Electric* v. *Gilbert*, 429 U.S. 125 (1976).

[10] Karen O'Connor, *Women's Organizations' Use of the Courts* (Lexington, Mass.: D.C. Heath, 1980), 144-145.

to End Discrimination Against Pregnant Workers (Campaign). Because the original court case was brought by the International Electrical, Radio, and Machine Workers Union, the IUE, AFL-CIO, UAW, and other union groups were prominent in this struggle, although the issue was of paramount importance for women's activist groups such as NOW, WEAL, NWPC, and the WRP of the ACLU. The coalition's leadership was drawn from the original litigating groups; Ruth Weyand of the IUE, who had argued the case before the Supreme Court, and Sue Ross of the ACLU-WRP were elected co-chairs.

The Pregnancy Disability Act (S. 995), to amend Title VII of the Civil Rights Act of 1964 to include pregnancy-related disability, was introduced in Congress by Senator Harrison Williams in March 1977. A "Fact Sheet" distributed by the Campaign set "the parameters of legislative debate. Little time was spent discussing the logic of the *Gilbert* decision. Congress began to deal directly with the circumvented issue."[11]

The intent of the Act was to prohibit discrimination against pregnant women in all areas of employment including hiring, firing, seniority rights, job security, and receipt of fringe benefits. It also required employers who offered health insurance and temporary disability plans to provide coverage to women for pregnancy, childbirth, and related medical conditions.

Feminist groups were opposed more overtly on this issue than they had been on credit by some industry groups including the U.S. Chamber of Commerce, National Association of Manufacturers, National Retail Merchants Association, American Retail Federation, and insurance companies. Nonetheless, industry did not present monolithic opposition to pregnancy-related disability insurance. Businessmen's objections, as expressed in hearings, centered on the view that pregnancy is a "voluntary condition," not an illness, hence not liable to the same coverage as other disabilities. In addition, they cited the potential for increased costs. Even so, the

---

[11] Greenwald, "Women's Rights," 28.

business community was clearly not unanimous in its opposition to this bill since such leading corporations as Xerox, Polaroid, and IBM already provided pregnancy-disability coverage for their employees. Also, as in the case of equal credit opportunity, some business groups were reluctant to go on record against the feminist community, particularly on an issue involving "motherhood." The Supreme Court winners— General Electric, Liberty Mutual, AT&T, and others—did not testify, although invited to do so, at the Senate hearings held in April 1977.[12]

At both the House and Senate subcommittee hearings held in April and June 1977, feminist groups and their allies provided testimony stressing the importance of change. Several women who had been personally victimized by discriminatory insurance plans offered dramatic commentary on the necessity for remedial legislation. The proposed legislation enjoyed unusually broad-based support even from pro-life forces (specifically the American Citizens Concerned for Life) who welcomed the proposed legislation as a "matter of social justice" and supported rights of pregnant "mothers" as a logical extension of their concern for life. Conflict began to occur when the Bishop's Committee for Pro-Life Activities sought the addition of language eliminating elective abortions from the definition of covered conditions, as part of their broader strategy to generate anti-abortion support in every way possible. In the Senate Thomas Eagleton (D–Mo.) introduced an anti-abortion amendment to the Pregnancy Disability Act. Feminists were especially dismayed because they had thought incorporation of pro-life groups in the Campaign's coalition would prevent such action. Nonetheless, the bill passed the Senate in September 1977 by a vote of 75-11, with its initial definition of covered pregnancy-related conditions intact. Senator Eagleton's anti-abortion amendment was defeated.

The issue of pregnancy disability then moved to the House where controversy regarding anti-abortion language contin-

---

[12] *Ibid.*, 30.

ued and was heightened. Representative Beard (D–R.I.) introduced the anti-abortion amendment in the House. At this time issues such as extension of the ERA and the Humphrey-Hawkins Full Employment Bill occupied the attention of many Campaign coalition members. Nonetheless, coalition action and cohesion were maintained. Member organizations were asked to visit key legislators during home recesses. A postcard campaign in support of the bill was launched. Action/information pieces were distributed by the Campaign and by NOW-LDEF. Wide media (television and newspaper) exposure was obtained to focus attention on the bill.

In February 1978 the House subcommittee chaired by Representative Augustus Hawkins (D–Calif.) marked up H.R. 6075 rejecting the Beard anti-abortion amendment by two votes; on March 13, 1978, the full committee overruled the subcommittee, adopted the Beard amendment by seven votes, and then voted 25-6 to report out the bill to the floor of the House as amended. During the next five months the Campaign maneuvered to remove the amendment or obtain a floor vote under a "suspension of the rules." Eventually, the House leadership decided to bring H.R. 6075 up under "suspension of the rules," a procedure normally used to expedite noncontroversial legislation. Bills called up under this procedure may have no amendments from the floor and must be passed by a two-thirds vote.[13]

The House leadership and leaders of the Campaign supported this strategy as a way to move the bill to conference committee where they hoped it might be possible to eliminate the anti-abortion amendment. This strategy created an unusual split among pro-choice forces; NARAL, NOW, and the Religious Coalition for Abortion Rights opposed this tactic, wishing to put supporters and opponents "on the record," although they muted overt disagreement. The ACLU and NWPC and other women's rights groups favored "suspension" in an effort to prevent a floor fight that they felt they would surely lose and that would result in a damaging symbolic defeat. The

[13] *Ibid.*, 35.

New York Times, editorializing at the time, said: "We recommend, albeit sadly, a vote for the amendment" because of the necessity to gain passage of the legislation rectifying abuse against pregnant women.[14]

In the House roll-call vote on the issue, some "no" votes were registered in opposition to the anti-abortion language as well as to the pregnancy-disability act itself. The bill with the anti-abortion Beard amendment passed the House by a vote of 376-43. The bill then went to conference committee where pro-choice forces were reunited and where conferees were deadlocked all summer over the language of the bill.

House conferees voted consistently in favor of the Beard amendment provisions and against Senate conferees' compromise language, supported by pro-choice forces, which would allow religious institutions to deny abortion coverage to their employees.[15] House conferees rejected Senate conferees' efforts to broaden the so-called conscience clause language to include sole proprietors with religious or moral objections to abortion. Finally, on October 12, 1978, a compromise emerged. Pro-choice forces agreed to compromise by including some anti-abortion provisions, in order to gain the larger objective of securing the passage of the Pregnancy Disability Act.

The final language approved by the conference committee and sent back to the House and the Senate for approval allows employers to exempt elective abortions from medical coverage, except if the life of the mother is threatened or if medical complications result from abortion. But, in a minor weakening of the original House anti-abortion provisions, employers were required to provide disability and sick-leave benefits to women recovering from abortion. The Act does not specify an absolute ban on employer provision of abortion benefits; employers may provide all health benefits related to abortion if they wish. Both houses of Congress passed the bill and the President signed it. The law took effect immediately upon passage, on October 31, 1978, with the exception of fringe

[14] *New York Times*, July 18, 1978, 16.
[15] *CQ Weekly Report*, Oct. 21, 1978, 3073.

and insurance benefits, which took effect 180 days after enactment.

Pro-choice and feminist groups welcomed the passage of the Act as a milestone for the women's movement, but pro-choice groups in particular remained bitter over what they viewed as the "betrayal" of Representative Augustus Hawkins (Chair of the House Subcommittee), who had orchestrated the original compromise on suspending the rules. Pro-choice forces felt that Hawkins's efforts to strike the Beard provisions proved less than zealous and that House and Senate conferees had sought continuing approval from the United States Catholic Conference on various compromise proposals.[16]

Conclusion

The passage of the Pregnancy Disability Act after twenty-two months of Congressional debate contains within it several paradoxes. Feminists, pro-choice groups, and their allies in the unusually broad-based Campaign to End Discrimination Against Pregnant Workers achieved their goal of the Act's passage, overturning a Supreme Court decision within a relatively short period of time. Even the Court itself may have responded to pressure generated by feminist groups. In a related case, *Nashville Gas Co. v. Satty*,[17] the Supreme Court seemed to adopt a position somewhat different from that in *Gilbert* when it held that employer policies of denying accumulated seniority to women returning from maternity leave violated Title VII of the Civil Rights Act of 1964, although the Court did hold that a policy of not awarding sick-leave pay to pregnant employees was not prima facie evidence of sex discrimination. Nonetheless, the campaign almost faltered, but not because of opposition from the business community whose interests were most directly at stake, as might have been anticipated. In fact, business groups were split on

16 *Ibid.*, 3074.
17 98 S. Ct. 347 (1977).

the issue, despite the fact that no industry groups actually testified in support of the bill. The Act almost failed because of the activities of pro-life groups, who threatened to divide the members of the Campaign and weaken their unity, thus destroying the coalition and chances for the bill's passage.

The efforts of pro-lifers did not succeed, but there was disagreement within Campaign ranks over appropriate strategies and even over ultimate worth of the bill. Pro-choice groups, especially NARAL, which has a single-issue mission, of necessity see their interests as being somewhat different on such a policy controversy from those of broader-based feminist groups. Although their focus on this issue differed considerably, the feminist/labor strategy of compromising in order to win what they saw as the larger issue prevailed. The final bill, other than the anti-abortion language, does represent a sweeping victory for feminist forces; even an earlier section of the bill, delaying implementation of the Act for smaller companies, was deleted from the final version. In addition, the broad language of the original bill, which contains a sweeping definition of areas of employment in which discrimination is outlawed, prevailed. It should be recalled that the compromise version of the abortion language in the Act does permit optional provision of abortion coverage by employers and also requires that the costs of complications arising from abortions in all cases be covered. This represents a softening of the initial Beard amendment language. The National Conference of Catholic Bishops, understandably, was not pleased with the law and the EEOC guidelines issued to enforce it and brought suit in Federal Court challenging the Pregnancy Disability Act. The suit was dismissed by Judge John Pratt of the U.S. District Court on the grounds that no new issue suitable for adjudication had been presented.[18]

The Pregnancy Disability Act broadens equal opportunity protection for millions of working women, while serving as

[18] *Chronicle of Higher Education*, Feb. 4, 1980, 16.

a reminder of the price of compromise that had to be paid in order to obtain this important victory. Although it is still too early to assess compliance with the new Act, it provides a legislative mandate that guarantees women pay for their period of disability and a comparable job upon their return.

CHAPTER 8

THE FEMINIST MOVEMENT:
THE PAST AND
LIKELY FUTURE

INTRODUCTION

Our analysis has suggested that when issues are perceived as affecting role equity rather than role change, the opportunities for favorable impact on the political system have been maximized for feminist groups. It has further been proposed that when the feminist movement has experienced success in attainment of policy goals, this has been due in large measure to keen understanding of the realities of the American political system and adherence to the four rules outlined in Chapter 1.

We have argued that several factors are crucial to attainment of goals in the American political system: these include an issue with the image of broad-based support; an issue narrow enough not to challenge basic values or divide supporters; a policy network with access, and capability of providing information, to decision makers; the willingness to compromise with constituent groups and in the political process; and, finally, the ability to define success in terms of increments of change rather than total victory.

In this final chapter we will evaluate the utility of the distinction between role equity and role change as two poles of a continuum and the validity of the four rules proposed. In addition, we will venture a look at the prospects for continued feminist participation in politics.

167

THE POLITICS OF CHANGE

Perhaps the most sweeping change created by the activity of women lobbyists in the policies considered here occurred in the Equal Credit Opportunity Act, which operating in a policy vacuum created new policy in an area potentially affecting millions of women. However, although women did succeed in broadening the political agenda, they did so only by conforming to the system's "mobilization of bias." The issue was relatively noncontroversial, involving distributed costs and distributed benefits. While business may incur greater costs, they will be passed on indirectly to the the consumer, and both women and men may profit, for example, from the extension of mortgage credit to a two-income family. Issue demands were specific and challenged no fundamental societal values. Though ultimately a redistributive issue in the sense that it transfers economic power to women, this policy was perceived as one of equity or equal rights and as such had no formal opposition. The issue did not involve mass publics and was resolved at the leadership levels of politics. The absence of a national precedent to rely upon facilitated possibilities for innovation.

The Pregnancy Disability Act was similarly a relatively narrow issue, one involving no public outlay of funds. Like the Equal Credit Opportunity Act, this legislation dealt with equitable treatment for women—in this instance, clarifying the precise meaning of sex discrimination against women under Title VII of the Civil Rights Act of 1964. However, since the issue dealt with pregnant women and therefore the potential role of women as mothers and homemakers, it was fraught with more controversy than the Equal Credit Opportunity Act, particularly since the question of funding abortions under disability plans received vociferous attention from opponents of "free choice." Nonetheless, backed by a coalition of over three hundred groups, from labor unions to Right to Lifers, and even some business groups, the legislation enjoyed broadbased support. No doubt some supporters of pregnancy disability legislation view this policy area as encouraging pro-creation and family development and, therefore, as being consistent with "pro-family" politics. The demands were highly specific and narrow and, like the credit issue, involved little intervention from outside the federal policy-making structure itself. Thus it is not surprising that women enjoyed success on this issue—although they did have to compromise on the issue of abortion as a pregnancy-related disability.

For Title IX, banning sex discrimination in schools, the issue of role change was more clearly involved. More overt disagreement arose regarding the degree to which the federal government should go on prohibiting policies and practices that treated the sexes differently in educational institutions. A major controversy arose around the issue of intercollegiate sports for women, which involved the maintenance of traditional sex roles for women. Other issues seemed to have strong sexual overtones, related to fears of potential invasion of privacy, and created hostile reactions from members of Congress and administrative officials including then HEW Secretaries Casper Weinberger and Joseph Califano. In contrast to the speed and ease with which the Equal Credit Opportunity Act moved through the political rulemaking process, Title IX took seven years, and even at that, compliance with the Act is uneven and challenges continue to occur in the political arena, in courts, and on campuses.

Of all the issues considered here, abortion is the one that most involves role change, because it is perceived as having the most impact on women's roles as wives and mothers and most appears to threaten traditional societal patterns. Because of the ideological nature of the abortion issue, feminists have suffered numerous defeats in the legislative process. Abortion is perceived to have consequences at the ballot box. Virtually all members of Congress and lobbyists agree that the most mobilized pressures come from the pro-life groups, who have created the impression that they represent single-issue voters who can cause electoral defeat for legislators who oppose them. Senator Robert Packwood of Oregon, who opposes the ban on federal funding for abortion, has called abortion a single issue that could destroy a congressman's career because of the strong feelings it generates.[1] An important question for the women's movement is whether erosion of support on the abortion issue (and possibly ERA as well) will cause a spillover and create a negative atmosphere in which to sustain and add to gains made in the more narrow role equity areas. However, as our analysis of responses from those we interviewed has suggested, feminist issues are perceived as separable by legislators, largely owing to the specialized, issue-focused orientation of the feminist movement, and for this reason it is likely that defeat in one policy area will not result in defeat on other, narrower issues.

THE RELEVANCE OF THE PLURALIST RULES

In the preceding pages it has been suggested that a number of variables have helped determine the success or failure of feminist women acting through interest groups in the federal policy-making process.

A major factor that influences success is the image of broad-based support. On each of the issues considered, women have established coalitions with different but overlapping membership bases—in order to maximize resources and effectiveness. Examples include the pro-choice caucus, the Campaign to End Discrimination Against Pregnant Workers, and the National Coalition for Women and Girls in Education.

Another factor is the selection of narrow issues that do not challenge basic values or divide potential supporters. We have seen that on issues that are narrow and that focus on role equity, activity by women's rights groups has found considerable support. Since the congressional passage of the ERA, Congress has been receptive to those women's issues that have little organized opposition in order to appeal to feminist constituents who may play a role in members' reelection.

[1] *New York Times*, Oct. 6, 1977, 16.

When more dominant values are in question and role change issues regarding women's family and dependent status are at stake, the possibilities for success become severely limited. The media and congresswomen—to cite two groups generally supportive of women activists on both the Equal Credit Opportunity Act and the Pregnancy Disability Act—have been split, as has society generally, on such issues as federal funding for abortions.

The existence of a policy network, which has internalized the values of feminist lobbies and includes within its ranks members of the decision-making system, is supportive of women activists. The policy network that has been formally institutionalized in Washington includes representatives from the legislative and administrative sectors of government and the media, as well as legal and professional women in the nation's capital. As a result of this network, crucial information (feedback) regarding the status of proposed policies has clearly enhanced the position of feminists in policy making.

Receptivity to feminist issues has been aided by the existence of a caucus of women members of Congress, to which all women representatives belonged in the 95th Congress. These women have collectively supported most women's issues other than abortion. Congressional aides and administrators in bureaucratic roles contribute to group effectiveness as well. In the administrative policy-making sector, as one recent study has pointed out, well-organized groups that monitor an agency and mobilize expertise in support of policy change may sometimes "counter-balance the considerable financial resources of industries and well-established groups."[2] In the case of the Equal Credit Opportunity Act and Title IX, the impact of monitoring by newly mobilized and active organizations contributed to success. The Equal Credit Opportunity Act demonstrated the ability of women's organizations to influence the regulatory process in a new policy area.

[2] Paul Sabatier, "Social Movements and Regulatory Agencies: Toward a More Adequate and Less Pessimistic Theory of Clientele Capture,". *Policy Sciences* 6 (1975), 320.

Internally, women's groups have made more effective use of limited resources by developing specialized interests and dividing areas of specialization and by being flexible in choosing what strategy to employ in specific instances. Although several groups, such as NOW and WEAL, tend to be multi-issue organizations, we have seen that different groups have specific policy predispositions (such as NARAL in its coordination of activity on the abortion issue). High-level research and legal expertise are available to women activists from such groups as CWPS, ACLU-WRP, CLASP-WRP, NOW-LDEF, and WLDF, and these groups have provided vital assistance to activist women on all the policy issues considered here, though constrained in lobbying activity because of their tax-exempt status. Personal lobbying of sympathetic and interested legislators and bureaucrats has been increasingly utilized as newly sophisticated women's groups are involved in making "head counts" of supporters and opponents' strength. Constituency pressure, in the issues studied here, has also been used as a backup resource, to be mobilized in order to demonstrate adverse women voters' reactions to recalcitrant legislators and administrators.[3] Increased efforts by women's rights groups and their allies to maintain records on legislative voting for specific issues and disseminate information to constituents in order to defeat anti-feminist elected officials may prove effective in future electoral campaigns. Litigation also is used in conjunction with traditional lobbying techniques in order to influence the outcome of national policy.

Successful groups also serve to provide informational resources to bureaucrats and members of Congress. In each of the policies considered here, women have concentrated primarily on providing technical expertise through testimony in Congress and written comments in the regulatory process. For example, during the formulation of the Equal Credit Oppor-

---

[3] It should be noted that neither partisanship nor traditional support for liberal civil rights legislation necessarily is predictive of legislative voting on most women's issues. Republicans—including Brock, Packwood, and Brooke—have been active in supporting various women's rights policies.

tunity Act, legislators and administrators called upon women activists to legitimize their own support of a given decision as well as to supply political intelligence and to provide important data. According to the recent analysis of politics at the Office of Civil Rights, HEW: "To this day, the most detailed and comprehensive public record of OCR rulings under the Title IX regulations is not a government publication but the newsletter of the National Organization of Women (NOW) Project on Equal Educational Resources (PEER)."[4]

In each of the policies under consideration here, the women activists showed themselves ready to accept less than total victory. With regard to the Equal Credit Opportunity Act and the Pregnancy Disability Act, women compromised in their legislative demands and, regarding the ECOA, in their regulatory demands.[5] Women activists involved in Title IX lobbying accepted compromise on several notable occasions, too, by acceding to narrow exemptions to the law in order to forestall greater limitations.[6] On the abortion issue, activist women have been willing to concede the near impossibility of "victory" in releasing federal funds for abortions; they have concentrated their efforts instead on seeking the vaguest, fuzziest legislative language possible in order to permit the largest number of poor women to gain funded abortions, on working through the judicial process, and increasingly on building grassroots support.

Success is usually defined as incremental, and both group tactics and image must be perceived as legitimate. In none of the cases examined here was confrontation the chosen strategy. The tactics of women's groups have been centrist and

[4] Jeremy Rabkin, "Office of Civil Rights," in James Q. Wilson, ed., *The Politics of Regulation* (New York: Basic Books, 1980), 329.

[5] Although as of March 1977, owing to legislative lobbying, primarily from other "rights" groups, many original feminist demands relating to the ECOA were met.

[6] Rabkin also makes this point with specific reference to exemptions for father/son, mother/daughter events from Title IX ("Office of Civil Rights," 335).

traditional, conforming to the system's "mobilization of bias." In evaluating the tactics adopted by women, an analysis of abortion politics in Hawaii seems relevant: "The appeal was reasonable, low key and essentially conservative," despite the radical degree of change entailed. Tactics appealed to reason, assuming legislators would decide on the merits of the issue, and stressed traditional middle-class values.[7]

Similar findings are reported by Janet Boles, who found in her study of the ratification process for the Equal Rights Amendment that, for the most part, ERA "proponents excelled in traditional interest group politics" and were particularly successful at the Congressional level, where they were able to discuss the issue in legalistic terms and present its abstract and technical meaning.[8]

Several concluding observations about the movement itself seem necessary. The women's movement has become professionalized and bureaucratized in the past several years. However, despite these developments, which often can lead to organizational rigidity, the groups that are involved with feminist political activity have not ossified. Quite to the contrary, the feminist movement has gained momentum and has engaged in new initiatives and strategies. The early emphasis of the movement on the concept of "sisterhood" has remained a unifying force, with the result that *inclusivity* remains an operating principle. Disparate groups have been accepted into movement politics.[9] The commitment of feminist activists remains movement oriented, negating the role of "media stars" or charismatic leaders, as has occurred in some other types of reform groups, and preventing organizational demise with the departure of key individuals. We have suggested that women activists possess limited resources but relatively high status.

[7] Patricia Steinhoff and Milton Diamond, *Abortion Politics: The Hawaii Experience* (Honolulu: University Press of Hawaii, 1977), 210.

[8] Janet Boles, *The Politics of the Equal Rights Amendment* (New York: Longman, 1979), 123, 171.

[9] Carolyn Teich Adams and Katherine Teich Winston, *Mothers at Work* (New York: Longman, 1980), 133.

They are professional activists who relate to mass constituencies that may be mobilized to demonstrate electoral (political) clout. Leaders and members are largely white, middle-class women[10] who possess significant levels of technical competence.

THE PARAMETERS OF CHANGE:
THE LIMITS OF FEMINIST IMPACT

This book has sought to demonstrate the importance the newly mobilized feminist movement has come to assume in several key policy areas dealing with the role of women in contemporary society. Nonetheless, it should be emphasized that not all benefits—legislative and other—for women have emanated from pressure brought by organized groups. The passage of the Equal Pay Act of 1963, although it represented the enactment of a demand made by women's groups for decades, predates the onset of an organized feminist movement. The anti-sex discrimination clause of the Civil Rights Act of 1964 was inserted as a "joke" by a Southern representative who hoped that its frivolous inclusion would weaken the entire bill's credibility.[11] And, although the case for feminist impact may be made most convincingly for the period beginning in 1970, not all gains in this period reflect massive pressure-group activity by feminists. Occasionally other factors, including the lack of opposition and the narrowness of an issue, have been sufficient to gain passage of needed legislation. Such success without massive expenditure of resources is a testament to the degree of acceptance feminists have gained in politics.

It must be emphasized that by 1980 the feminist movement

[10] Both Maren Lockwood Carden and Jo Freeman have stressed this aspect of the women's rights movement. See Maren Lockwood Carden, *Feminism in the Mid 1970's* (New York: Ford Foundation, 1977), 99-121, and Jo Freeman, "Women and Public Policy" (unpublished manuscript), 27-28.

[11] See Adams and Winston, *Mothers at Work*, 121, for elaboration of this point.

had gained widespread acceptance as a legitimate pressure group. Testimony to this was provided by the federal government's funding of the Houston Women's Conference in honor of the International Women's Year, held in 1977, and by the unprecedented congressional extension of the period for state ratification of the ERA for another three and a half years. By 1980 the Virginia Slims American Women's Opinion Poll revealed a heightened perception of sex bias in economic-based activities and substantial increase in women's holding of mortgages, credit cards, and other financial arrangements in their own right.[12] It would appear that recognition of the equity-related issues is growing, and this reflects both an awareness of the impact of the feminist movement and a base for its continued political activity.

The impact of any movement for social change is difficult to gauge. On the one hand, as we have suggested, numerous sex-related barriers for women in society had eroded by 1980. Several signs, on the other hand, indicate how far the feminist movement still has to travel. Among the key problems remaining are several that are economic in nature, including a *declining* median income for women relative to men (coupled with greatly increased labor force participation and increased economic opportunities) and continuing sex-related occupational segregation.[13] Thus, whereas in 1955 women on the average earned 63.9 percent as much as men, in 1978 women's average earning capacity was down to 59.4 percent of men's. Moreover, this decline in relative earning power occurred during a time when women in increasing numbers were joining the nation's work force and men's and women's educational attainment levels were the same. In 1955, of all women over

[12] *1980 Virginia Slims American Women's Opinion Poll* (New York: Roper), 15, 96-97. A 1973 Redbook poll revealed 66 percent of readers favoring the women's movement; quoted by Carl Degler, *At Odds* (New York: Oxford University Press, 1980), 448.

[13] See Adams and Winston, *Mothers at Work*, 2-3; and Ronnie Steinberg Ratner, *Equal Employment Policy for Women* (Philadelphia: Temple University Press, 1980), 12-23.

the age of 16, 35.7 percent were in the labor force; in 1979 the comparable figure was 51 percent. In 1955 women represented 31.6 percent of the total labor force; in 1979 our nation's work force was 42.2 percent female. Occupational discrepancies explain some of the income differentiation. Although 43.3 percent of all professional and technical workers in the United States are women, only 12.4 percent of relatively well-paid lawyers and judges are women; and 96.8 percent of all registered nurses and 84.3 percent of all elementary teachers—notoriously poorly paid professions—are women. Furthermore, although over 84 percent of elementary teachers are women and 50.7 percent of secondary teachers are women, only 37.5 percent of school administrators are women. If this latter figure is disaggregated among the more prestigious and well-paid positions—especially secondary school principals—there are an insignificant number of women.[14]

Another measure of the continuing necessity for change is that despite increased social acceptance of work for women, the role of women in home and family has remained much the same. Numerous writers have pointed to the dual—economic and domestic—roles shouldered by most women and to the limited change that has taken place in primary responsibility for the family, which still rests largely with women. The passage of equal employment legislation and litigative efforts by feminists have thus far resulted in only a limited government effort to aggressively alter patterns of sex bias that might significantly change economic roles for masses of women. In any event, even guaranteeing equal employment practices may have no impact on family roles, which often mirror in microcosm women's subordinate societal roles. Hence key problems for the future remain in the policy areas we have described as *role change* issues, which clearly redistribute power and resources to women, often in a highly politicized, conflict-

---

[14] U.S. Department of Labor, Women's Bureau, Office of the Secretary, *Employment Goals of the World Plan for Action: Developments and Issues in the United States* (Washington, D.C.: U.S. Government Printing Office, 1980), 10-11, Appendix A, and Table 10.

laden political setting. Recognition of the nature of these problems suggests the accuracy of the view that only narrow, *role equity* issues may gain ready acceptance in the contemporary political system.

The politics of the ERA, an issue that appeared at the congressional level to be the very apotheosis of role equity, has now engendered profound opposition and massive counterpressures from those who fear its broader implications. As the anti-ERA groups are linked to anti-abortion and other conservative forces—now joined with "pro-family" groups as well—continued confrontation seems inevitable. It is interesting to ponder the likely effects of the failure of the pro-ERA forces to garner enough support in the states for the ultimate inclusion of the Amendment in the Constitution. Though failure to win approval of the ERA will be demoralizing for the women's movement, it should be expected that the organizational diffuseness of the movement will serve to maintain its viability. Thus the multiple activities and successes related to equity questions will keep the movement alive. In addition, as more laws affecting equity roles are enacted and as more rights for women are protected by the law, sufficient momentum will be sustained to keep the movement a viable force in American politics. The cumulative effects of role equity changes at some future time may well have the effect of creating role change.

To date, the women's movement has made limited use of the courts, in part because of the uneven response of the judiciary to questions dealing with sex discrimination. However, during the past two decades there have been some positive responses by the judiciary on issues dealing with women's equality. Gender-based classifications were found to be unconstitutional in several cases—*Reed* v. *Reed*[15] and *Frontiero* v. *Richardson*.[16] In *Taylor* v. *Louisiana*[17] automatic jury exemptions based solely on sex were declared unconstitutional.

[15] 404 U.S. 71 (1971).
[16] 411 U.S. 677 (1973).
[17] 419 U.S. 522 (1975).

Several provisions of the Social Security Act were held invalid, when they differentiated on the basis of sex in the provision of benefits, in *Weinberger* v. *Weisenfeld*[18] and *Califano* v. *Goldfarb*.[19] The Supreme Court held unconstitutional mandatory termination of employment for pregnant women in *Cleveland Board of Education* v. *La Fleur*.[20] Title VII's sex-discrimination provisions were the subject of considerable litigation in the federal courts. In *Phillips* v. *Martin Marietta Corporation*[21] the refusal of employers to hire women with pre-school-age children was held unconstitutional. In *Dothard* v. *Rawlinson*[22] the Supreme Court found that a seemingly neutral job qualification relating to height and weight in effect denied equal opportunity to women and was unconstitutional. Despite these rulings that favor women as a group, others, such as *Kahn* v. *Shevin*,[23] perpetuate unequal treatment of women before the law. If the ERA should fail, the courts nonetheless might be one avenue of redress that the women's movement might use to greater advantage.

Finally, despite conservative countermovements, the states are likely to become more central arenas for the women's movement. Of course, the impact of feminists varies from area to area as organization and prevailing political culture differ. To date, state-based legislative and other policy-oriented efforts often have been successful. Sixteen states have enacted equal rights amendments, for example. States have often been leaders in efforts to free marriage and divorce laws from sex-based stereotypes, to use one's own choice of surname, to gain fairer laws dealing with sexual assault, and to aid displaced homemakers.

The 1980 elections marked the first time since authoritative election polls were begun in 1952 that a wide gap in voting

[18] 420 U.S. 636 (1975).
[19] 97 S. Ct. 1021 (1977).
[20] 414 U.S. 632 (1974).
[21] 400 U.S. 542 (1971).
[22] 97 S. Ct. 2720 (1977).
[23] 416 U.S. 351 (1974).

appeared between the sexes. Women split their vote virtually evenly between Carter and Reagan, while men supported Reagan with 54 percent of their vote (to 37 percent for Carter).[24] An ABC News General Exit Election Poll found a significant difference between men's and women's votes for Carter based on desire to remain out of war and on the Equal Rights Amendment, with more women aged 30-39 citing Reagan's stand on the ERA as their reason for voting against him than any other single issue (32 percent).[25] Nonetheless, despite the emergence of a potential women's bloc vote, the election of 1980 proved disastrous. With the defeat of President Carter, who supported many feminist goals, and the ouster of many leading defenders of feminism in the Senate, and their replacement in both instances by opponents of free choice and the ERA, the prospect even for new equity-related legislation appears poor.

Still, a record number of women were elected in 1980 to Congress and to state and local legislative positions. Although many of these women are not feminists, it is well to recall a 1977 study done by the Center for American Women and Politics at Rutgers University. The study found that, regardless of ideological identification, women legislators of both parties took more feminist positions on issues such as abortion, the ERA, child care, and social security for homemakers than did their male counterparts.[26] Without asserting that such survey results may necessarily translate into public policy, we can at least say that the potential for building upon the already established "policy network" described throughout this volume obviously exists.

It is possible that the upheaval caused by the November 1980 elections will galvanize feminists and their supporters into greater organizational efforts.[27] A reevaluation of strat-

[24] *New York Times*, Nov. 9, 1980, 28.

[25] *ABC News General Exit Election Poll*, Tables 6, 8 and 18. Data made available by Jeffrey Alderman, Director, ABC News, Political Unit.

[26] *New York Times*, Nov. 4, 1980, B8.

[27] *New York Times*, Nov. 7, 1980, A16.

egies may well be in order, and grassroots organizing efforts may be identified as more essential tools for influencing policy. It is also possible that the coming decade will see more emphasis on cementing gains already made, by continued monitoring of the commitment of administrative agencies to enforcement of existing laws.[28]

The flexibility with which strategies for influencing policy are employed by feminists will continue. The strategy that may have the most profound long-term effect is the expansion of the movement from leadership-based lobbying efforts to constituency-based organizations—though to date the constituency groups such as NOW and NARAL have small memberships compared to the size of their potential constituencies. Grassroots electoral activity, first attempted on a major scale in 1980, may, in conjunction with expanded membership cadres, also prove to be important and may facilitate expanded influence for women's groups. Effective impact on issues such as employment and child care will need to involve more women workers themselves in feminist politics, a trend only in its incipient stages.

An overriding problem for the entire feminist community is funding. Thus far, financial resources have limited the scope of activity for the organizations considered in this volume. Unless financial opportunities increase, political participation may not be able to expand. Women's organizations have entered politics largely at the policy-making stage. Until 1980 their activity was not, as just noted, focused on electoral activity. Certainly additional funding would facilitate such activity and might foster additional successes. Feminists have made significant gains in the federal policy-making process, but their continued efforts to achieve broad change in established societal roles must contend with the numerous obstacles our political system has erected at every turn.

[28] Timothy B. Clark, "After a Decade of Doing Battle, Public Interest Groups Show Their Age," *National Journal*, July 12, 1980, 1140-41.

THE FUTURE OF FEMINIST POLITICS

We have seen that for women activists, there are no easy victories, but considerable success may be achieved by intensive organizational intervention—at all stages of the decision-making process, including the implementation stage. Incremental policy making tends to prevail, although it is our contention that issues perceived as narrow in scope may have a profound impact on the role of women in society. If the women's movement continues to abide by the "political rules of the game" and if parameters are drawn around issues selected for advocacy, so that opposing groups are muted, feminists will continue to be successful political participants in an age of declining parties and pluralist expansion of interest-group politics.

APPENDIX 1: INTERVIEWS

The materials for the case studies were derived in large measure from interviews with leaders of feminist groups, congressional and administrative decision makers, and staff assistants. Many feminist leaders were interviewed at least twice—once for organizational information and once for policy-oriented information. Interviews lasted from one to three hours and were often followed by telephone conversations. They were conducted from 1975 to 1979.

A list of persons interviewed (with the affiliations they had at the time of their interview) follows as does a list of questions (in Appendix 2).

Abshire, Pat – Staff, Senate Banking and Currency Committee, Washington, D.C.

Bailey, Barbara – Aide to Representative Ed Koch, Washington, D.C.

Beck-Rex, Marguerite – Executive Director, SPRINT, Washington, D.C.

Benshoof, Janet – Staff Attorney, ACLU-RFP, New York

Berresford, Susan – Program Officer, Ford Foundation, New York

Brown, Cindy – Deputy Director, OCR, HEW, Washington, D.C.

Bryce, Rev. Edward M. – Director, Pro-Life Office, National Conference of Catholic Bishops, Washington, D.C.

Bucher, Jeffrey – Federal Reserve Board of Governors, Washington, D.C.

Burris, Carole – Director, Women's Lobby, Washington, D.C.

Campbell, Sharyn – Staff Attorney, Bank Americard and NOW Task Force on Credit, Washington, D.C.

Chapman, Jane Roberts – Director, CWPS, Washington, D.C.

Clohesy, Stephanie – Executive Director, NOW-LDEF, New York

Cooper, Ranni – Associate Director, Women's Campaign Fund, Washington, D.C.

Cox, William – Director, National Committee for a Human Life Amendment, Washington, D.C.

Dickson, Barbara – Aide to Senator Birch Bayh, Washington, D.C.

Dornan, Robert – Congressman, Washington, D.C.

Dubrow, Evelyn – Lobbyist, ILGWU, Washington, D.C.

Dunkle, Margaret – Staff Attorney, HEW, Washington, D.C.

Flemming, Arthur – Director, U.S. Commission on Civil Rights, Washington, D.C.

Gates, Margaret – Co-Director, CWPS, Washington, D.C.

Ginsberg, Ruth Bader – Professor of Law, Columbia University, founder and Adivsory Committee member, ACLU-WRP, New York

Glasser, Ira – Director, ACLU, New York

Glickstein, Howard – Professor of Law, Howard University, Washington, D.C.

Gold, Sally – Staff Attorney, Federal Trade Commission, Washington, D.C.

Goldfarb, Lewis – Staff Attorney, Federal Reserve Board Task Force on Credit, Washington, D.C.

Goldsmith, Judy – Vice President, NOW, Washington, D.C.

Gordon, Robin – Director of Public Relations, PEER, Washington, D.C.

Hart, Janette – Deputy Director, Federal Reserve Board, Office of Savings and Consumer Affairs, Washington, D.C.

Hartnett, Cathy – Associate Director, Voters for Choice, Washington, D.C.

Heagstedt, Nina L. – Legislative Assistant, NOW, Washington, D.C.

Howitt, Idell – Staff Attorney, Federal Reserve Board Task Force on Credit, Washington, D.C.

Holstein, Charles – Aide to Representative Leonore Sullivan, Washington, D.C.

Appendix

Koch, Edward – Congressman, New York
Kohn, Margaret – Staff Attorney, CLASP-WRP, Washington, D.C.
Kramer, William – Attorney, Squire, Sanders & Dempsey (counsel to NCAA), Washington, D.C.
Law, Sylvia – Professor of Law, New York University, ACLU-RFP Advisory Committee, New York
Leitzer, Ellen – Staff Attorney, ACLU, Washington, D.C.
Lichtman, Judith – Director, WLDF, Washington, D.C.
Lipson, Linda – Director, Congressional Clearinghouse on Women's Rights, Washington, D.C.
Loukas, Helen – Staff, U.S. Commission on Civil Rights, Washington, D.C.
Malcolm, Ellen – Staff, NWPC, Washington, D.C.
Middleman, Michael – Deputy Assistant Director, OCR, HEW, Task Force on Athletics, Washington, D.C.
Miller, Kathy – Staff, ACLU, Washington, D.C.
Mulhauser, Karen – Executive Director, NARAL, Washington, D.C.
Neier, Aryeh – former Director, ACLU, New York
Northrup, Graham – Staff, House Financial Institutions Subcommittee, Washington, D.C.
Norton, Eleanor Holmes – Chair, EEOC, Washington, D.C.
Novick, Lee – Aide to Representative Bella Abzug, Washington, D.C.
O'Donnell, Anne – Director, Right to Life Committee, Washington, D.C.
Parr, Carol – Executive Director, WEAL Fund, Washington, D.C.
Paul, Eve – Legal Director, National Planned Parenthood Federation, New York
Peratis, Kathleen – Executive Director, ACLU-WRP, New York
Picker, Jane – Founder, Board Member, Women's Law Fund, New York
Pinzler, Isabelle Katz – Director, ACLU-WRP, New York
Polikoff, Nancy – Staff, CWPS, Washington, D.C.
Polivy, Margot – Counsel to AIAW, Washington, D.C.

185

Rauh, Joseph – Attorney, Rauh, Silard & Lichtman, Washington, D.C.

Ross, Susan – Professor, George Washington University Law School, Washington, D.C.

Sandler, Bernice "Bunny" – Director, Project on the Status and Education of Women, Association of American Colleges, Washington, D.C.

Segal, Phyllis – Legal Director, NOW-LDEF, New York

Shack, Barbara – Attorney, New York Civil Liberties Union, New York

Smith, Delores, Federal Reserve Board, Washington, D.C.

Steele, Celia – Staff, NOW-LDEF (PEER), Washington, D.C.

Tatel, David – Attorney, Hogan and Hartson; former Director, OCR, HEW, Washington, D.C.

Thornton, Maureen – Legal Staff, LWV, Washington, D.C.

Werner, Carol – Staff, NARAL, Washington, D.C.

APPENDIX 2: QUESTIONNAIRE

For Groups

1. What is your average annual budget?
2. How many people are employed in your office—in professional and other capacities? What is the percentage of attorneys on the staff?
3. How was your group created: a) an issue, b) an individual, c) a crisis, d) split off from another group, e) other?
4. Is your source of funding largely from a) membership dues, b) foundations, c) the U.S. government or other governmental sources, d) other? Which foundations are your major donors?
5. Is your organization dominated by its board or professional staff in terms of policy making? How is the board selected?
6. Please give an example of how one specific policy strategy was determined. How was the decision-making process structured?
7. Does your office allocate most of its resources to: a) lobbying, b) research, c) publicity, d) litigation, e) monitoring the political process, f) testifying before Congress and the executive branch, g) constituency lobbying, h) other? Explain.
8. Are you a membership organization? If yes, how many members do you have? Do you have local chapters? How many and where?
9. Do you participate in coalitions with other groups? With which groups are you most closely associated? Is your relationship with it/them structured or informal?
10. How would you assess your organization's effectiveness?

11. On what issues has your organization had the most impact?
12. What strategy used by your organization has had the most impact: a) lobbying, b) litigation, c) publicity, d) protest, e) monitoring, f) testifying, g) other?
13. What is your tax status: 501(c)(3) or (c)(4)? What is your relationship with groups that have another tax status?
14. Is there one dominant figure within your organization—within the feminist political community?
15. Does one group play a dominant role in feminist politics? Which one?
16. Does your organization specialize in a particular issue area?

FOR INDIVIDUALS

1. Why did you seek out a career in feminist politics?
2. What is your background, education, career training? Law degree or other advanced degree?
3. What is your current salary?
4. What is the nature of the job you perform?
5. Do you desire to remain in your present job?
6. What is your assessment of your personal effectiveness?
7. What is your assessment of your group's effectiveness? Which techniques are most effective: a) lobbying, b) monitoring, etc.?
8. Does your group specialize in one particular issue area?
9. Which other groups are you closest to politically? What is the nature of your relationship?

INDEX

ABC News General Exit Poll, 180
abortion: background, 126-130; division of groups on, 12, 134-138, 170; federal funding for, 130-137, 143, 145, 153-164, 168-170; litigation on, 33, 132-135. *See also* Hyde amendment; pro-choice, abortion groups; pro-life movement
Abortion Information Exchange, 146
Abzug, Bella, 53, 85, 132
academic discrimination, 31, 98-100. *See also* education rights
Ad Hoc Committee in Defense of Life, 145
Adams v. *Califano*, 116
administrative positions for women, 99, 155-158, 176-177
administrative process and women's rights, 79-81, 117-118, 171
AFL-CIO, 160
alimony, 69
Alyeska Pipeline Service Co. v. *Wilderness Society*, 45
American Association of University Professors (AAUP), 103
American Association of University Women (AAUW), 20, 25, 27, 76, 99, 103, 146
American Bankers Association, 83
American Citizens Concerned for Life, 144, 161
American Civil Liberties Union (ACLU), 26-27, 32-34, 44, 46, 53-54, 146-151, 162, 172

American Council on Education (ACE), 60, 103
American Medical Association (AMA), 146
American Retail Federation, 160
Americans for Conservative Action, 72-73
Americans for Democratic Action, 72-73
amicus curiae briefs, 55, 158
Anderson, John, 148-149
anti-abortion amendment, 144-146, 153, 162
anti-abortion legislation, 126-128, 144, 162-166
anti-war movement, 141, 144
Ash, Roberta, 24
Association for Intercollegiate Athletics for Women (AIAW), 26-27, 60, 104-106, 121
Association of American Colleges' Project on the Status and Education of Women, 103-104
athletic guidelines, 27, 31, 55, 96-97, 104-107, 118-120, 123-124. *See also* intercollegiate athletics
attorney's services for groups, 45, 53-55

banks, 68, 81, 83-85
Bayh, Birch, 85, 96, 108, 131, 139
Beal v. *Doe*, 133
Beard, Edward, 154
Beard amendment, 137n, 154-164
behavioral patterns of groups, 9-13, 37-39, 174

Belloti v. *Baird*, 150
Bergmann, Barbara, 62, 85
Bernard, Jesse, 32, 62
Berresford, Susan, 47
Berry, Jeffrey, 42
birth control, *see* contraception
Bishop's Committee for Pro-Life
  Activities, 161
Bishop's Pastoral Plan, 142, 144
blacks, 137, 146-147. *See also* civil
  rights
Bloomingdale's Department Store,
  92-93
Boles, Janet, xiv, 174
Brock, William, 72-74, 77
Brooke, Edward, 131, 135
Brown, Cindy, 111-112, 117-118
Bryce, Edward M., Rev. 142
Buchanan, Allen, 39
Bucher, Jeffrey, 81, 85
bureaucratization, 23-25, 174-175
Burns, Arthur, 84-85
Burris, Carole, 29n, 76
business and credit, 81-84, 103;
  and pregnancy disability, 161,
  168. *See also* credit industry
Business and Professional Women
  (BPW), 20

Califano, Joseph, 116, 118, 122,
  133-134, 169
Califano v. *Goldfarb*, 179
campaign groups, 9, 28
Campaign to End Discrimination
  Against Pregnant Workers, 160,
  162, 164, 170
Campbell, Sharyn, 70, 74
Cannon v. *University of Chicago*,
  117
Card, Emily, 73
Carden, Maren Lockwood, 7n, 22
Carnegie Corporation, 46
Carter, Jimmy, 133, 146, 180
Casey, Robert, 109-110

Catholic Charities, 144
Catholic Church, 129, 137-140,
  142-146, 153
Catholic League for Religious and
  Civil Rights, 144
CBS News/*New York Times* polls,
  142-143
Center for American Women and
  Politics, 180
Center for Constitutional Rights,
  149
Center for Law and Social Policy
  (CLASP), 26, 33, 41, 55, 57, 60-
  62, 103, 172
Center for Women's Policy Studies
  (CWPS), 26, 32-33, 36, 41, 48,
  56-57, 70-71, 75-78, 80, 82, 90,
  172
Central-Charge, 90
Chafe, William, 16
Chapman, Jane Roberts, 41n
child care, 6, 18-20, 53, 181
Child Health Assurance Program
  (CHAP), 136
child support, 69
Children's Bureau, 156
Christian Family Renewal, 140
Church, Frank, 139
civil rights movement, 16, 18-19,
  22, 25, 29, 32-33, 37, 46-47, 51,
  53, 59, 80, 102, 107-108, 110,
  112, 146-147, 155
Clark, Dick, 138-139
Clark, Peter, 17
class-action suits, 72-74, 149-150
class struggle, 145-146
Cleveland Board of Education v.
  LaFleur, 179
Coalition for Reproductive Rights
  of Women, 60
Coalition on Women Appointments, 60
coalition politics, 5, 20-21, 25-27,
  54-55, 58-63, 83, 89-90, 95-96,

103-105, 108, 111-114, 116-120, 122, 128-130, 134-152, 154-165, 168-170. *See also* networking
Coalition to End Discrimination Against Pregnant Workers, 60
Cohen, Linda, 84-85
Columbia University Law School, 57
Commercial Credit Corporation, 91
Committee for Abortion Rights and Against Sterilization Abuse (CARASA), 146
Committee for the Survival of a Free Congress, 140
Common Cause, 23, 144, 146
Comprehensive Child Development Act of 1971, 6
compromise, 64, 86-90, 124, 136-140, 163-167, 169, 173-174
Congress: and abortion, 130-140, 180; and credit, 62-80, 84, 172; and educational rights, 96-98, 107-110, 122, 124, 169, 173; and pregnancy disability, 158-164
Congressional Black Caucus, 147
Congressional Clearinghouse for Women's Rights, 140n
Congressional Quarterly, 137-138
Congressional Women's Caucus, 138, 171
consciousness-raising, 19, 54
Consumer Credit Survey, 91
consumer rights, 80-85
Consumer's Union, 76
Conte, Silvio, 132
contraception, 18, 68, 87
cosmetics industry, 48
Cox, William, 144
Cracking the Glass Slipper kit, 58, 114
credit discrimination, 6-7, 11-12,

59, 66-72, 80-81, 88-89, 91, 130-131, 160-161, 176. *See also* Equal Credit Opportunity Act of 1974
credit industry, 71, 81-84, 86-87

day care, *see* child care
DeCrow, Karen, 70, 84
Democratic party, 149
Des Moines Register, 139
direct-mail solicitation, 43
divorce, 18, 67-69, 88
doctors and abortion, 127-128, 134, 146
Dooling, John F., Jr. (Judge), 149
Dornan, Robert, 136, 141
Dothard v. *Rawlinson*, 179
Dresner and Tortorello, 151
Drinan, Robert (Father), 137

Eagleton, Thomas, 161
Economics and Discrimination Project (University of Maryland), 85
Edna McConnell Clark Foundation, 46
Education Amendments of 1972, 95, 122; of 1974, 102, 107
education programs of groups, 49
education rights, 6-7, 11-12, 53-55, 60, 95-115; background, 98-101. *See also* athletic guidelines; Title IX
Education Task Force, 103
elderly, 59
elections: and abortion, 138-140, 148-150, 153; and women's rights, 179-180
electoral groups, 9, 27-29
emergent groups, 10-11
enrollment in schools, 99-100
Equal Credit Opportunity Act (ECOA) of 1974, 5, 7, 56, 59, 63-65, 74-79, 81, 89-90, 92-94, 103, 154, 168-169, 171-173

Equal Employment Opportunity Commission (EEOC), 42, 158, 165
Equal Pay Act of 1963, 5, 175
Equal Rights Advocates, 32n
Equal Rights Amendment (ERA), 6, 15, 20, 25-31, 52-53, 59, 71, 80, 90, 149, 162, 170, 174-180
Evans, Sara, 21
Executive Order 11246 (1965), 6
Executive Order 11375 (1967), 6

Fair Housing Act of 1974, 6
family role of women, 18-19, 89, 96, 130, 152-153, 167-171, 177. *See also* role change
Federal Depositories Insurance Bill, 74
federal funding of abortions, 130-137, 143, 145, 155-164, 168-170; of education, 109-110. *See also* Title IX
Federal Reserve Board, 63-64, 70-71, 78-89, 91-93; Office of Saver and Consumer Affairs, 64, 85, 93
Federal Trade Commission, 92; Bureau of Consumer Protection, 93
feminism: defined, 4; history, 14-24; impact of, 175-182
feminist groups: funding, 42-50, 181; genesis, 3-4, 14, 18-24; membership, 27-28, 50-52; staff, 39-42; structure, 24-25, 29-36, 174; techniques, 52-62, 173-174, 180-181; types, 4, 26-28. *See also specific groups*; coalition politics; single-issue groups
fetal rights, 129-130
Field Foundation, 46
flexibility of groups, 38, 49, 52, 61-62, 181. *See also* compromise
Flood, Daniel, 151
football, 96-98, 121

Ford, Gerald, 109, 132
Ford Foundation, 33, 46-50, 55, 70
foundation grants, 46-50
Freeman, Jo, 16, 21, 65, 175n
Friedan, Betty, 17, 19, 22
Friends for Life, 145
fringe benefits, 156-158
Fritz, Sara, 84
Frontiero v. *Richardson*, 54, 178
funding for groups, 42-50, 181
fund-raising events, 45-46
Furness, Betty, 66

Gallup polls, 143, 152
Gardner, John, 23
Gates, Margaret, 62, 76-77
Gedulig v. *Aiello*, 158
General Counsel's Office, 107
General Electric v. *Gilbert*, 54, 154-155, 157-164
General Federation of Women's Clubs (GFWC), 20, 29, 58
Ginsburg, Ruth B., xiv, 62
Girl Scouts, 103
Goldfarb, Lewis, 81, 93
government grants, 43
Grant, Christine, 118
grassroots organizations, 36, 51, 75-76, 111, 129-130, 140-144, 146-153, 173, 181. *See also* mass constituencies
Green, Edith, 96, 100, 102, 108
Greenberger, Marcia, 41n, 104
Greer, Germaine, 19
Griffiths, Martha, 53

Haener, Dorothy, 85
Harris, Patricia R., 116, 120-121, 122
Harris v. *McRea*, 54, 159
Hart, Janette, 64, 85
Hawkins, Augustus, 164
Health, Education, and Welfare,

Department of, *see* U.S. Dept. of
    Health, Education, and Welfare
health issues and feminism, 33. *See
    also* abortion; pregnancy
Heckler, Margaret, 53, 73-76
Helena Rubenstein Foundation, 48
Helms, Jesse, 136
hierarchies, 22-24. *See also* leader-
    ship behavior
H——L—— v. *Matheson*, 150
Holt, Marjorie, 108
Holtzman, Elizabeth, 53, 86n
Horbal, Krysten, 62
House Committee on Banking and
    Currency, 66-67, 76-77
House Committee on Post-Second-
    ary Education, 110
House-Senate Conference Commit-
    tee, 107
House Subcommittee on Consumer
    Affairs, 66, 74-77
House Subcommittee on Financial
    Institutions, 77-78
House Subcommittee on Labor and
    Health, Education, and Welfare,
    110, 151
Houston Women's Conference, 176
Humanae Vitae, 142
Humphrey-Hawkins Full Employ-
    ment Bill, 162
Hyde, Henry J., 131
Hyde amendments (1976-1979), 7,
    54, 56-57, 130-137, 140, 144,
    150, 158

IBM, 161
*Impact of the Hyde Amendment on
    Federally Funded Abortions*
    (1978), 57
Impact, 80, 148
"in kind" services, 45
In the Running, 56, 116
incentive theory, 17-18, 39-41
incest, 133-136

inclusivity, 174
income, 67, 174-177
incremental issues, 9-11, 38-39, 64,
    167, 173
information distribution by groups,
    10, 52, 56-57, 173
insurance industry, 161, 168
intercollegiate athletics, 96-101,
    104-105, 112-114, 118-124, 169
interest-group theory, 8-13, 15-18,
    24, 38, 39, 40, 42, 79-80, 138,
    167. *See also* role change; role
    equity
interlocking directorates, 61-62
Internal Revenue Service (IRS), 55,
    80
International Union of Electrical,
    Radio, and Machine Workers
    (IUE), 159-160
International Women's Year
    (1977), 59, 140, 176
Interstate Association of Commis-
    sions on the Status of Women,
    74

Jackson, Jesse, 147
Javits, Jacob, 107, 118
Jews, 142
Johnson, Lyndon, 100
Judicial Selection Panel, 60
Junior League, 34

Kahn v. Shevin, 179
Kanter, Rosabeth, 22
Kellogg Foundation, 46
Kingdon, John, 138
Koch, Ed, 75-77
Kohn, Margaret, 41n, 62, 104
Komer, Odessa, 62
Knox, Holly, 41n, 119

labor force, women in, 18, 67-68,
    155-158, 176-177, 181

Index

labor unions, 60, 146, 155, 159-160, 168-169
Landau, Brooksley, 62
Law, Sylvia, 62
Lawyers Committee for Civil Rights under Law, 34
leadership behavior, 4, 15-18, 21-24, 39-42, 52, 58-61, 174-175, 181
Leadership Conference on Civil Rights, 146
League of Women Voters (LWV), 20, 25-27, 28n, 58, 90, 103, 147
Leahy, Patrick, 136
legislative process and women's rights, 5-6, 53-57, 59, 64-80, 101-102, 172. See also Congress
legitimacy of groups, 9-10
lesbians, 22
Liberty Mutual, 161
Lichtman, Judith, 34, 60, 62
Life Amendment Political Action Committee (LAPAC), 139-140
life endangerment and abortion, 132-136, 150, 163
Life-letter, 145
"Life Lobby," 144
Lipson, Linda, 140n
litigation and women's rights, 4-5, 10, 31-35, 45, 49, 52-53, 117-118, 122, 132-135, 149-151, 153, 172-173, 178-179
loans, 85, 88. See also credit; mortgages
lobbying, 5, 9, 33-36, 52, 172; and abortion, 136-140, 142-146, 153; and ECOA, 55-58, 71, 74-80; and Title IX, 102-111, 115-122

Maher v. Roe, 133
male sports establishment, 96-98, 103, 105, 118-122
"March for Life," 140, 144

marital status, 18, 67-69, 87-88
mass-based groups, 4, 9, 26, 29, 38-39, 50-52, 58, 122, 140-144, 148-151, 155, 167, 170-172, 175, 181
mass group behavior, 4, 29-31, 122
Massey, Patricia, 76
material incentives, 17-18, 39-40
maternity leave, *see* pregnancy disability
Mathias, Charles, 136
Matthews, Forrest D., 116
maximum liability, 72, 89
MBA programs, 99
McCormack, Ellen, 140
McGovern, George, 139
media use, 41, 64-65, 69, 84, 122, 162-163, 171
Medicaid, 131-138, 149
medical school, 99
membership dues, 43-45
methodology of research, 6-13
Michels, Robert, 24
Millett, Kate, 19
minorities, 42, 46, 59
mobilization of bias, 3, 10, 63, 89, 168, 174
Moe, Terry, 8n, 17, 39
Moffett, Robert, 141
monitoring by groups, 55-57, 90, 113-115, 122, 124, 171, 181
Moral Majority, 139
Mormons, 139, 142
mortgages, 67-68, 92, 168, 176
Moses, Margaret, 62
Mott, Stewart, 147
Ms. Foundation, 46
Mulhauser, Karen, 41n, 57n

Nadel, Mark, 80
Nader, Ralph, 23
Nashville Gas v. Satty, 164
National Abortion Rights Action League (NARAL), 15, 25-28, 35-

36, 43-45, 50, 57-58, 132-134, 139, 146-151, 162, 165, 172, 181
National Advisory Council of Women's Educational Programs, 115
National Association for the Advancement of Colored People (NAACP), 29, 146; NAACP Legal Defense and Educational Fund, 32, 35, 53
National Association of Manufacturers, 160
National Association to Repeal Abortion Laws, *see* NARAL
National Bank Americard, 74
National Coalition for Women and Girls in Education, 60, 103-105, 111-114, 116-120, 122, 170
National Coalition's Task Force on Enforcement, 104
National Collegiate Athletic Association (NCAA), 55, 98, 102, 103, 105-106, 112-113, 118-123
National Commission on Consumer Finance, 69, 73
National Committee for a Human Life Amendment, 143
National Committee on International Women's Year, 85
National Conference of Catholic Bishops, 142-143, 165
National Conservative Political Action Committee (NCPAC), 139
National Council of Jewish Women (NCJW), 25-27, 75-76
National Education Association, 155
National Federation of Business and Professional Women's Clubs, 76
National NOW Times, 29
National Organization for Women (NOW), 15, 20-30, 43-48, 50,

52; and abortion, 146-147, 151; Bill of Rights (1967), 30; and ECOA, 58, 67n, 70, 75-77, 82-83, 87; Legal Defense and Education Fund (NOW-LDEF), 25-26, 29, 34-45, 43-46, 48, 55, 57, 104, 162, 172; and pregnancy disability, 160, 162; Task Force on Consumer Credit, 70, 75, 83-85; and Title IX, 130
National Retail Merchants Association, 160
National Right to Life Committee, 141-146
National Women's Political Caucus (NWPC), 20, 26-31, 36, 44-45, 50, 66, 75, 103, 146, 160, 162
networking, 20-21, 25-28, 40-41, 58-62, 139, 148-151, 159-164, 167, 170-175, 180. *See also* coalition politics
new left movement, 18-20
New York Foundation, 46
New York Times, 84, 92, 148, 162
Nineteenth Amendment, 14

Obey, David, 134
O'Donnell, Anne, 145
Office of Civil Rights of HEW (OCR), 96, 98, 103, 105-106, 110-117, 121-123, 173
Olson, Mancur, 17, 38, 39, 40
Omnibus Education Amendment, 102
Onaitis, Susan, 83
"Operation Push," 147
Orfield, Gary, 79-80

Packwood, Robert, 131, 169-170
PEER Perspective, 116
Phillips v. *Martin Marietta Corporation*, 179
Picker, Jane, 28n
Pilpel, Harriet, 62

Planned Parenthood, 146-151
*Planned Parenthood of Central
Missouri* v. *Danforth*, 150
Playboy Foundation, 46
pluralist theory, 63-64, 170-175
Polaroid, 161
Polikoff, Nancy, 76
political action committees (PACs),
27, 29, 36, 144-146, 148-150
Polivy, Margot, 104, 113n
Pope Pius IX, 142
Pratt, John, 117, 165
pregnancy disability, 6-7, 11-12,
59-61, 154-165
Pregnancy Disability Act of 1978,
5, 7, 54, 56, 61, 137n, 154-165,
168-169, 171, 173
prison reform, 22
privacy, 134, 149, 169
pro bono legal services, 34, 45, 53-
55
pro-choice abortion groups, 6-7,
11-12, 51, 56-57, 60, 125-153,
163-164, 170
Pro-Life Action Committee, 139,
141
pro-life movement, 36, 51, 58,
125-155, 159-160, 165, 168-
170, 180
professionalization of groups, 14-
15, 31-35, 37-42, 174-175
Project on Equal Education Rights
of NOW (PEER), 26-27, 29, 35-
36, 46, 56-58, 104, 114-115,
173
Protestants, 142
protests as technique for change,
52-53, 151
Proxmire, William, 85
public opinion and women's rights,
14-15, 66, 142-146, 151-152,
176, 180
purposive incentives, 17-18, 40-41

quickening, 126

radicalism, 19-20
rape, 133-136
Reagan, Ronald, 180
Redbook, 152
Reed v. *Reed*, 33, 54, 178
Regulation B (ECOA), 82, 88-91
Rehnquist, William, 159
Religious Coalition for Abortion
Rights (RCAR), 148, 151, 162
religious groups, 137-146
Reproductive Freedom Project
(ACLU), 25-26, 33-34, 47, 54,
57, 148
Republican party, 49
research, 4, 10, 52, 56-57, 122
"Respect Life" Sunday, 144
retail industry, 83-84
Richardson, Elliot, 116
Riggs National Bank, 90
right-to-life movement, *see* pro-life
movement
Rockefeller Brothers Fund, 46
Rockefeller Foundation, 46
Rockefeller, John D., III, 34, 46
Roe v. *Wade*, 129-131, 140, 150
role change, 7-8, 10-11, 89, 96,
130, 152-153, 167-171, 177
role equity, 7-8, 10-11, 64-65, 89,
96, 123-124, 152-154, 160-171,
178

Salisbury, Robert, 16-17
Sandler, Bernice "Bunny," 62, 104
Sanford, Terry, 119
Schattschneider, E. E., 3, 10
Scheidler, Joseph, 145
scholarships, 101, 104, 124
Scott, Ann, 76
Sears, Roebuck Co., 83
Segal, Phyllis, 35

Senate Appropriations Committee, 108
Senate Banking Committee, 85
Senate Labor and Human Resources Committee, 155n, 157
sexual freedom, 18, 22, 125
Shanahan, Eileen, 85
single-issue groups, 4, 10-11, 26-27, 35-36, 112, 139-146, 165, 167, 169-170, 172, 181-182
single women, 68-69
Skerry, Peter, 125
social fraternities and sororities, 108
social-movement theory, *see* interest-group theory
Social Security Act, 54, 179. *See also* Title XIX
solidary incentives, 17-18, 40-41
Solomon, Fred, 85
specialization of groups, 26, 61, 63, 95
SPRINT (WEAL), 27, 31, 56-57, 104, 116
staffing of groups, 39-42
Stalled at the Start, 56, 114-115
state funding of abortion, 137-138
state legislation and women's rights, 179-180
Steele, Diana, 62
Steinem, Gloria, 22, 62
Stokes, Louis, 147
Sullivan, Leonor, 74

Tax Reform Act of 1976, 6
taxes and interest groups, 26, 80
Taylor, Emily, 85
Taylor v. Louisiana, 178
television and sports, 106
Third National Conference of State Commissions (1966), 19
Thompson, Carolyn, 141
Thornton, Maureen, 28n

Tilly, Charles, 16
Title VI of the Civil Rights Act of 1964, 50-51, 96, 107
Title VII of the Civil Rights Act of 1964, 6-7, 45, 54, 59, 154, 156, 158, 160, 164, 168, 179
Title IX of the Education Amendments of 1972, 5, 7, 11, 27, 29, 31, 33, 36, 46, 55-58, 95-124, 169, 171-172
Title XIX of the Social Security Act, 133, 136
"To Your Credit," 93
Tower, John, 107
traditional women's groups, 4, 14-15, 20, 25, 27-29, 39, 52, 58-62, 64, 76, 103, 146
Truman, David, 15
Truth in Lending Act, 72-73
turnover: in groups, 41; in labor, 68-69

Unenforced Law: Title IX Activity by Federal Agencies Other Than HEW, The, 115-116
United Auto Workers Union (UAW), 160
United Press International, 84
United States Catholic Conference, 164
U.S. Chamber of Commerce, 160
U.S. Commission on Civil Rights, 42, 121, 123, 137n
U.S. Department of Education, 111, 121, 124
U.S. Department of Health, Education, and Welfare (HEW), 43, 55-56, 80, 96-97, 107-114, 116-124, 132-135
U.S. Department of Housing and Urban Development (HUD), 92
U.S. Department of Justice, 93
U.S. Department of Labor, 109

U.S. Department of State, 42-43
U.S. Office of Education, 43
U.S. Supreme Court, 5, 45, 53-54, 117, 128, 132-133, 140, 150-151, 154-155, 157-164
University of Michigan, 14
Urban League, 29

viability of the fetus, 129
violence and pro-life groups, 145
Virginia Slims American Women's Opinion Poll: 1974, 66, 91; *1980*, 14, 176
Volkmer, Harold, 136
Voters for Choice, 27, 28n, 148

War Manpower Commission, 156
Washington Council of Women Businessowners, 86
Washington Women's Network, 60
WEAL v. *Califano*, 55, 61, 116, 118
WEAL v. *Weinberger*, 108
Weber, Max, 24
Weinberger, Caspar, 116, 169
Weinberger v. *Weisenfeld*, 54, 179
welfare, 54, 138-140, 146, 152
Wendt, Diane, 118
Weyand, Ruth, 159-160
Weyrich, Paul, 140
White House Conference on the Family (1980), 140
Widnall, William, 76

widowed women, 68-69
Williams, Harrison, 160
Williams, Wendy, 155n, 157
Wilson, James Q., 17, 79
Women's Bureau (Dept. of Labor), 68
Women's Campaign Fund, 28, 29n
Women's Educational Equity Act (WEEA), 43, 95, 115
Women's Equity Action League (WEAL), 20, 25-28, 31-32, 42-46, 48, 50, 55-57, 60-62, 75, 100, 103-104, 116, 128, 159
women's groups, *see* feminist groups *and* traditional women's groups
Women's Law Fund, 28n, 32n
Women's Legal Defense Fund (WLDF), 25-28, 34, 42-45, 51, 55-58, 60-62, 159-160, 172
Women's Lobby, 29n, 75-77, 146
Women's Political Times, 31
Women's Rights Project of ACLU (WRP), 26, 33, 44, 45, 54-57, 60, 62, 103, 159-160, 172
Women's Rights Report, 56
"Women's Strike for Equality," 52
World War II, 155-156

Xerox, 161

Zald, Mayer, 24

Joyce Gelb is Associate Professor of Political Science at
the City College and the Graduate Center of the City
University of New York. Marian Lief Palley is Professor
of Political Science and Chairperson of the Department
at the University of Delaware.

Library of Congress Cataloging in Publication Data

Gelb, Joyce, 1940-
Women and public policies.

Includes index.
1. Women in politics—United States. 2. Feminism—
United States. 3. United States—Social policy.
I. Palley, Marian Lief, 1939- . II. Title.
HQ1426.G35   305.4′2′0973   82-400
ISBN 0-691-07639-1   AACR2
ISBN 0-691-02209-7 (pbk.)